designing costume
for stage and screen

designing costume
for stage and screen

Deirdre Clancy

Costume & Fashion Press/Quite Specific Media
An imprint of Silman-James Press, Inc.
Los Angeles

First published 2014
© Deirdre Clancy, 2014

The right of Deirdre Clancy to be identifed as author of
this work has been asserted by her in accordance with the
Copyright, Designs and Patents Act 1988.

Printed and bound by 1010 Printing International Ltd, China
for the publisher
Batsford
10 Southcombe Street
London W14 0RA
www.anovabooks.com

First published in the United States of America
By Costume & Fashion Press/Quite Specific Media
An Imprint of Silman-James Press Inc.
www.silmanjamespress.com
Info@silmanjamespress.com
(323) 661-9922 voice (323) 661-9933 fax

ISBN-13: 9781935247111

10 9 8 7 6 5 4 3 2 1

Contents

Introduction

Costume design is an ancient, ever renewing craft. Although one person is usually credited as the designer for performance costumes, the making of them involves many skills, each demanding different abilities and areas of expertise. This book seeks to both explain and honour these complementary arts.

Engaging the audience

Potential audience members will often phone a theatre's box office to find out if the production they are considering attending is set in period or traditional costume, because they don't expect to enjoy productions in contemporary dress nearly as much. Modern dress productions are sometimes thought of as less theatrical and potentially uncomfortable for all but the most sophisticated of urban audiences.

The costumes are often one of the first things an audience will discuss in the interval of a play. They are so powerful in making or marring any production, and if they are too showy, too dull, or just plain wrong, they can create an impenetrable barrier between the public and the performer; often, most members of the audience will not be able to pinpoint exactly what is making them unsettled. In classical theatre productions, one mark of a 'successful' costume is that of itself it is almost invisible, focusing the attention of the audience on the character. This can a difficult balancing act to achieve. Costumes need to be tactful without being boring, strongly attractive without getting in the way, and original without being silly – it's not easy.

Left A pencil design for the costume of Leonato from *Much Ado About Nothing*.

Right Lady Gaga is famed for the outlandish, attention-grabbing costumes she wears on stage.

Glamour

Of course, this somewhat old-fashioned, purist viewpoint absolutely doesn't apply to contexts where glamorous display is the whole point; where exuberance and rich design values are both demanded and appreciated. I explore this aspect of the art as well, looking at the wilder extremes of costume design, from eighteenth-century French ballet to the showgirls of Las Vegas and Broadway to the joyous excesses of singers such as Madonna and Lady Gaga.

Impact

Prior to the evolution of scenic design as we now know it, the constructed set was largely symbolic and depended on a limited range of theatrical properties. Under such circumstances, costume naturally assumed the principal role in defining the emotional world of the drama. To a much greater degree than is generally acknowledged, that remains true today, despite the best efforts of some critics to quash this idea!

Left A design for the character of Flora from the opera, *La Traviata*.

In fact, the moment that people put on any kind of costume or uniform, they are turned into performance artists. Whether on or off the stage, they move into a world of enhanced possibilities where they are no longer limited by the restrictions of everyday life. Costly embroidered vestments do not give a priest his position as an arbiter between God and mankind and a judge's robes do not confer his power of deciding a prisoner's fate, but the very fact of this visual differentiation bestows a kind of semi-magical power on the wearer. Think of royal regalia, for example. Put it another way: would Darth Vader be scary in bedroom slippers, or even in beige?

This book explores all that goes into the creation of performance costumes – the concepts, the crafts, the art, the beauty and the excitement. *Designing Costume for Stage and Screen* is generously illustrated throughout, often with designs and photographs by the author, and demonstrating a great variety of styles and genres through drawings, backstage glimpses and performance photographs.

Left The Dowagers from the opera *Eugene Onegin*.

Left above Fashion models from the Granville-Barker play, *The Voysey Inheritance*.

PART 1

From the Greeks to Lady Gaga

– a brief illustrated history

Mycenaean rituals

Above Minoan fresco depicting a leaping bull.

During the Mycenaean period (1600–1100 BC) in Greece, the cult of Demeter and her daughter Persephone demanded various rites and ceremonies. Based on the legend of the abduction of Persephone by the King of Hades and her rescue by her mother, week-long rituals centred around a symbolic narration of the story of the two goddesses and involved processions, animal sacrifice and getting high on sacred intoxicants (thought to be barley wine enhanced with magic mushrooms and laced with ergot). It is not difficult to relate this story to the yearly cycle and abundance or otherwise of the harvest.

The Minoan bull cult

In Crete, the Minoans' cult of the bull gave rise to exceedingly dramatic customs where young acrobats performed death-defying stunts in which they leapt over huge sacred bulls. This must have been as great and noisy a spectacle as the running of the bulls is today in Spain. The young men had very little in the way of costume, appearing to wear a small leather kilt and a waist-cinching corset made from reinforced leather. Long black ringlets, a leather cap and boots that resembled today's boxing or dance boots completed this surprisingly modern, very sexy look. The corset belt was probably made of hide, moulded and steamed into shape, and it offered some protection to vital organs from the horns of the bad-tempered bull. I do wonder what the mortality rate was.

Greek drama

Around the sixth century BC, the Greeks took the giant leap from fertility rituals to theatre as we might recognize it today: dramas of the emotions and behaviour of ordinary, if sometimes crazily extreme, people.

Greek drama was invariably played in masks. The theatres were so enormous that the basic expression of a character needed to be enlarged in order to be visible from the back. After all, few actors are especially noble or godlike (and none of them were women, who were almost entirely excluded from public life). Curiously enough, the masks were thought to protect the actors from the more malign aspects of their characters. Also, the masks' flared mouth parts may have acted as little megaphones that helped to project the actors' voices. Each 'type' had an instantly recognizable mask, ranging from gods and heroes to innocent virgins, wily slaves and my favourite, 'a harlot left off trade'.

The costumes utilized everyday garments such as the *chiton* or tunic and the *hemateon*, a cloak-like garment worn over the shoulders. These would have been made of dyed wool or linen and appear to have been decorated with traditional stencilled patterns. The gods and others playing tragic roles wore boots called *cothurni*, which elevated them above the other actors.

One startling aspect of costumes for popular comedy was the persistent use of the oversized phallus of red leather (probably a tradition inherited from earlier fertility rites). Since it must have been difficult to look at anything else, perhaps the very idea of being upstaged – so familiar to most actors – owes its origins to having to compete with a 60cm (2ft) leather phallus!

Fig. 1.

Fig. 2.

Fig. 3.

Fig. 4.

Fig. 5.

Fig. 6.

Fig. 7.

Fig. 8.

Fig. 9.

Fig. 10.

Drama in the Christian era: mystery plays

Given both the joyous and persistent use of sex on Greek and Roman stages and the fact that performers were considered to be on a level with prostitutes, it is hardly surprising that Christianity was totally hostile to all existing forms of theatre. Serious theatre almost died out during the first four centuries of the Christian era. Therefore there is a certain irony in the fact that it was the medieval Catholic Church that reanimated drama in the guise of Bible-based morality and mystery plays. Since few people could read their own language, never mind the Greek and Latin of the scriptures, the clergy found that the most effective way of teaching the stories and the morals of the Christian faith was to act out Bible stories in dramatic form.

Opposite Classical Greek actors' masks, used to show various expressions and emotions.

Below An Edward Bawden poster depicting scenes from the York Mystery Plays including The Adoration and The Risen Christ.

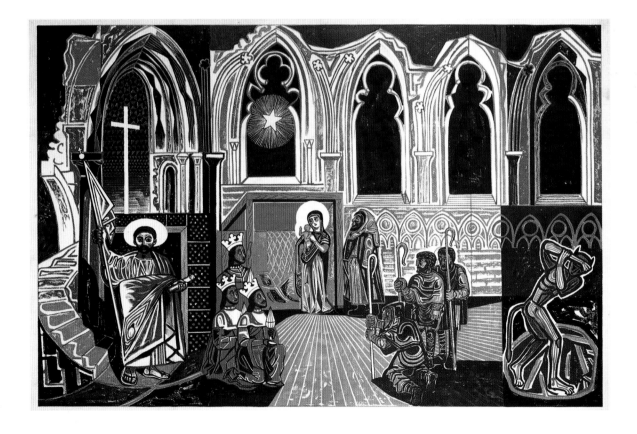

I consider it a logical inference that the large range of liturgical garments – a set of vestments in each of the seven liturgical colours owned by the churches – would have been adapted to dress angels and saints. One only has to look at the paintings and sculptures of the period to see that this would have made sense. Everyday clothes were used for secular characters; costumes of suede decorated with appropriately placed leaves (an early 'onesie', in fact) were used to simulate nudity; and performers might wear long wigs known as 'hairys', which were made of horsehair or human hair.

The origins of costume design: masques

By the fifteenth century, the religious displays of the Middle Ages had given way to more secular imagery. In a dramatic entertainment called a masque, masked performers played classical gods and legendary heroes such as Agamemnon and Cæsar, and were accompanied by dancers, singing boys and musicians dressed as nymphs, fauns and satyrs. Such processions, with their attendant banquets and firework displays, clearly featured an extremely high design content, not to mention top-class stage management skills. Figures representing qualities such as joy, hope or fear were carried over from the morality plays of the Middle Ages, but the classical element eventually prevailed, providing the excuse for ever more exotic costumes. (See also 'Inigo Jones')

Aery Spirit   Scogn Scolton   Roficros

Above Inigo Jones designs for figures
from the masque, *The Fortunate Isles*.

Commedia dell'arte

Below Henry Peacham's drawing of *Titus Andronicus*.

Opposite A female Harlequin figure in typically colourful dress.

Commedia dell'arte is a form of theatre which began in Italy in the sixteenth century characterized by masked 'types' and, for the first time in European history, featured women on stage. Originally the plays, based on well-loved stories or scenarios, were entirely improvised. Italian theatre historians, such as Roberto Tessari, and Luciano Pinto, believe commedia was a response to the political and economic crises of the time. It became the first entirely professional form of theatre funded by audience donations and, as such, was free to critique the current political situation. The commedia discovered a formula which both Hollywood and TV sitcoms, serials and soaps have since exploited to the full – the audience is able to identify with a range of immediately recognizable 'types' or characters, and their stories are given fresh impetus by constantly changing situations. Costume was essential to commedia dell'arte for the instant identification of the characters, Harlequin's diamond patchwork and the 'droopy drawers' of Pantalone (which persist in the word 'pantaloons') are obvious examples.

Shakespeare's time (1564–1616)

It is generally assumed that most actors wore a version of the fashionable dress of the day with appropriate additions. This is borne out by the sartorial anachronisms to be found in Shakespeare's texts. There is a well-known line in *Julius Cæsar* about 'sweaty nightcaps' being thrown in the air. The only known Shakespearean drawing is of a 1595 production of *Titus Andronicus* by Henry Peacham. This depicts a probably typical eclectic mixture of outfits. Note that Titus (holding the spear) is in a Roman toga, while Tamora, Queen of the Goths, wears Elizabethan dress, as do the soldiers behind Titus. We know that acting companies used elaborate costumes, but this drawing suggests that performances did not strive for historical accuracy. The figure on the right is the play's villain, Aaron the Moor.

A company's stock of costumes was of considerable value. Actors were in the habit of borrowing the more fashionable outfits for parties, and were fined if any were lost or damaged. Aristocrats would donate cast-off garments to their favourite players – an arrangement that conferred status on both parties. And once-used pageant and masque costumes also probably found their way into the wardrobe store.

Inigo Jones (1573–1672)

Inigo Jones was an architect, the designer of the Queen's House in Greenwich, and the favourite designer of James I. He was also the first British stage designer, who made sets of lovely drawings for his masques. Jones introduced a sort of classical Roman costume, which was to be a mainstay of the British stage for nearly two centuries.

The masque has its origins in a folk tradition where masked players would unexpectedly call on a nobleman in his hall, dancing and bringing gifts, on certain nights of the year or to celebrate dynastic occasions. The rustic presentation of a play within a play, *Pyramus and Thisbe*, as a wedding entertainment in Shakespeare's *A Midsummer Night's Dream*, offers a familiar example. Spectators were invited to join in the dancing.

Seventeenth-century baroque theatre

While spoken drama traces its ancestry from medieval morality plays, the lyric arts of opera and ballet evolved out of the pageants and masques of the Italian and French courts. The most extravagant of all King Louis XIV's spectacles was the great 1662 *Carrousel de Louis XIV*, in which it seems that every performer, musician and aristocrat, every artist, designer, dressmaker and craftsperson in the land played a part.

While comedies were usually played in costume that was an elaborated version of the fashions of the day, tragedies were usually set in an imagined classical time, but with bigger wigs and wider skirts.

Very few costumes survive from this period, but those that do are so thick with copper embroidery, sequins, braid and spangles (the better to reflect the limited, if flattering, power of candlelight) that the underlying

Below *Carrousel* performed by Louis XIV.

material is all but invisible. The clothes naturally became extremely heavy, and dancers would come off stage smothered in perspiration and sinking at the knees.

Some of these entertainments achieved a completely successful balance of the three theatrical forms – play, opera and ballet – reaching a peak with John Dryden's *The Fairy Queen* (music by Henry Purcell) of 1692. The story is a simplified version of Shakespeare's *A Midsummer Night's Dream*, in which each of the five acts contains a masque of very considerable scenic complexity. It demands huge resources, and even its 1692 premiere cost a massive £3,000 to stage.

Below A Jean Bérain design for the part of the Horseman with wings in *Le Carrousel des Galants Maures*.

English theatre after the Restoration

In 1642, one of the first acts of the newly empowered people's Parliament had been to close and later raze the theatres, the 'chapels of Satan'. It was the return of the court from exile in France in 1660 that created the characteristic Restoration style. (The explosion of creative talent after the Puritan Commonwealth was rather like the creative outburst in the 1920s after the grimness of the First World War.) Molière's style of commedia dell'arte inspired comedies of manners that became very popular, and playwrights such as Vanbrugh, Congreve and the first female dramatist, Aphra Behn, developed sophisticated English versions full of wit and sexual innuendo.

Meanwhile, the tradition of 'Roman' costume for classical subjects became rigidly stylized over the next two-thirds of a century. As companies and actors vied with each other for ever greater displays, armour grew in size and elaboration, as did the leading lady's dresses.

Above Penelope Keith and Robin Pearce in Congreve's *The Way of the World*.

Opera seria and opéra comique

Below An actress from 1898 dressed as the Wagnerian heroine, Brünnhilde.

Opera seria is an Italian musical term which refers to the noble and 'serious' style of Italian opera that predominated in Europe from the 1710s to c. 1770. With a few exceptions, opera seria was the opera of the court, of the monarchy and the nobility. Opera buffa was more likely to tell stories of less elevated folk, but was not necessarily especially humorous. Mozart's *Don Giovanni*, for instance is so classified, although it begins with a murder and ends with the Don being dragged down to Hell! Not very funny.

The term opéra comique is complex in meaning and cannot simply be translated as 'comic opera'. The genre originated in the early eighteenth century with humorous and satirical plays performed at the theatres of the Paris fairs which contained songs (*vaudevilles*), with new words set to already existing music, before morphing into the classic opera structure of sung arias which mostly reflected on the situation and the singers' 'inner life' and spoken recitatives. The style is thought to have evolved from the plays of the Commedia.

Below An actress from 1898 dressed as the Wagnerian heroine, Brünnhilde.

When I was at art school in the early 1960s, the ornate style of these operas was considered to be the pinnacle of the stage and costume designer's art. You could still see traditional opera and ballet productions at the Royal Opera House designed in this flamboyant way. As with the early Greeks, serious operas concerning gods and heroes were styled in archaic dress, with a fantastic version of Roman armour for the men (including the vastly overgrown *castrati*). The hero's helmet would be topped by towering ostrich feathers and his tunic, or *tonnelet*, was held out over cane panniers to echo the vast skirts of the ladies. Composers such as Mozart, on the other hand, were better known for comic operas such as *The Marriage of Figaro*, which would be dressed in heightened versions of contemporary dress.

NINETEENTH CENTURY

A real awareness of accurate period costume grew steadily under the influence of the historical self-consciousness brought about by the Gothick movement of the late eighteenth century. With the thirst for Shakespeare's original texts came a completely new approach to stage costume, where a quest for historical accuracy began to grow in significance.

Opera

A succession of great divas dominated opera from the mid-nineteenth century, and no male singer could match their popularity. Divas such as Jenny Lind, Adelina Patti and Nellie Melba amassed huge fortunes and flaunted them. Performing in Verdi's *La Traviata* at Covent Garden, Patti dismantled her jewellery and had the diamonds, valued at around £200,000, sewn on to the bodice of her costume. The effect was literally dazzling. Two policemen were borrowed from nearby Bow Street police station and mingled with the chorus on stage to keep an eye on them.

Opera at this time had no particular sense of unity in performance, despite a strong sense of stage design. The stars traditionally toured with their own costumes and often had scant regard for their colleagues and the composers. Rehearsals in the modern sense were unheard of, and star singers would rarely rehearse with the rest of the cast. In performance, the stars stood centre stage and ignored everyone else – even if singing a love duet with another star.

In Paris, the English couturier Charles Frederick Worth (1825–95) made a canny point of cultivating theatrical connections to publicize his firm. As a result, he was patronized by most of the leading artistes of the European theatre, including Sarah Bernhardt, Adelina Patti and Nellie Melba (who, being somewhat dumpy, must have been a bit of a challenge). This symbiotic relationship between dress designer and actress persists to this day, with the most glamorous actresses being offered the pick of the best collections to wear in the great free publicity parade along the red carpet leading to the Oscars.

Above Designs for Constanze in Peter Shaffer's *Amadeus*.

Left 1860s fashion design by Charles Frederick Worth.

Playwrights and actresses

Of the fathers of twentieth-century playwriting, only George Bernard Shaw (1856–1950) exhibited any interest in costume beyond its function as a dramatic signifier. He gave meticulous descriptions of his characters' clothes and, in researching Bulgarian uniforms and settings for *Arms and the Man*, used his very considerable draughtsmanship to produce what were, in effect, a set of costume drawings.

Ellen Terry

In productions of Shakespeare, the leading actresses were expected to provide their own costumes: Ellen Terry's well-known beetle wing gown, worn to play Lady Macbeth, is a good case in point. This costume is unusual in that we have the name of Terry's designer, Alice Comyns-Carr, and also (and this is almost unheard of) the costume-maker, Mrs Nettleship. There is not only a portrait by John Singer Sargent of Miss Terry wearing the gown, but also a photograph and, even more unusually, the much mended crochet gown itself, beetles' wings and all, survives and is on display at Terry's home, Smallhythe Place.

Dance costume

Usually, costume design reflects what is happening in fashion and fine art, adapting the spirit of the age to its own expressive needs, but for a few heady years at the turn of the twentieth century, stage design charged triumphantly into the lead with Léon Bakst's designs for the Ballets Russes.

Left The restored crochet dress with beetles' wings at Smallhythe Place.

Opposite Costume drawing by Léon Bakst for the ballet *Narcisse*.

PROGRAMME OFFICIEL
DES
BALLETS RUSSES

Costume de "NARCISSE"

Above Loie Fuller wearing one of her circle dresses, with the arms extended with canes.

An American dancer who should not pass without mention is Loie Fuller (1862–1928), who transformed herself into a thousand colourful images before the astonished eyes of her audience – with considerable help from her lighting designer.

Abstract costumes

Bauhaus designer Oskar Schlemmer's constructivist *Triadic Ballet*, conceived in 1912 but not premiered until 1922, sought to turn shapes into bodies; that is, to use dancers to animate static geometric designs. In this and other constructivist and cubist costume designs one feels the choreography is almost certainly secondary to the actual creations that the dancers are wearing. They are more than costumes, they are bizarre sculptural extensions of the body. It is significant that the costume designers of this school worked from an entirely masculine viewpoint and were almost always painters and sculptors who cared not a whit for the plastic expression of the dancers' bodies. However new and striking they must have appeared, they could just have easily been wheeled about on the stage by little robots, and must have been some of the most uncomfortable costumes ever invented. Many artists were commissioned to design ballets, including Pablo Picasso who designed Parade for Diaghilev's Ballets Russes.

Above Costumes designed by Oskar Schlemmer in a Bauhaus style for the Triadic ballet in 1926.

Showtime!

It may seem a violent gear change to leap from such advanced, high art ideas to the Ziegfeld Follies, but the link here is the extraordinary exotic and erotic costume constructions of Erté (1892–1990). Building his reputation as the leading cabaret-costume designer in his work for artists such as Josephine Baker, Romain de Tirtoff, the Russian designer known as Erté, was a wonderfully talented all-rounder, making costume designs, paintings, exotic sculptures, even lamps. He imbued even his sexiest dance costumes with haughty good taste, making the almost nude dancers look like duchesses. It was quite a trick, and his seriously classy work meant that over-excited husbands could safely take their wives, or more likely, their mistresses, to Erté's sophisticated shows at the Folies Bergère knowing it would be a great evening. Sexy without being vulgar is very hard to do, Brits and Yanks don't do it nearly as well as the French. And adding the witty, lissom form of Josephine Baker to the mix, the effect must have been electric.

Music hall, variety, vaudeville and the great British pantomime

If any forms of theatre celebrate national characteristics, they are to be found here. While the French had the elegance of the Folies Bergère, the British had music hall, vaudeville and pantomime – truly popular, and populist, theatre. Although Christmas pantomimes live on in a somewhat emasculated form, the arrival of television and film pretty much killed off demand. The heyday of these forms of theatre was from late Victorian times until the 1950s. Pantomime, in particular, attracted some of the best costume designers of the day, in particular Charles Wilhelm (or William John Charles) Pitcher (1858–1925).

Left Floral dress design by Charles Wilhelm.

Opposite Performer Josephine Baker wearing feathers to add to her onstage presence.

Above *Sleeping Beauty* with costume designs by Oliver Messel, revived in 2009 at the Royal Opera House, London.

What we think of today as classical ballet has its roots in the dance cultures of France and Russia. The iconic image of a slender ballerina *en pointe* (on point shoes) in a mid-length white net dress and little winglets attached to her shoulders, so familiar from traditional productions of *Les Sylphides* or *Giselle* was first seen illustrated by the great French ballerina, Marie Taglioni in the early nineteenth century. And interestingly the world wide language of the ballet is still French. However the first ballet school was Russian, the Imperial Ballet School in St Petersburg was founded in the 1740s. Ballet became highly popular with ordinary people through the provision of affordable, if uncomfortable, seating. In the UK we have cheap seats five balconies up called 'The Gods', while the Russian name for the same thing was 'Paradise Row'.

Serge Pavlovich Diaghilev had a great influence in shaping ballet's future. His greatest achievement was his dance company, the Ballets Russes. The productions of the Ballets Russes revolutionized early twentieth century arts and continue to influence cultural activity today.

But it is possible that revivals such as the Messel designed production of *Sleeping Beauty* would not have happened were it not for the brave and almost entirely forgotten dancer, Mona Inglesby. Her mentor Nicholas Sergeyev, ballet master of the Imperial Ballet School, realizing what was happening during the Bolshevik revolution of 1918, smuggled the irreplaceable dance 'scores' out of Russia, and brought them to the UK. Inglesby, then driving ambulances, and aged only 22, ran a full ballet company of 60 dancers that took ballet to unlikely venues all over war-torn Britain. (How, one wonders?)

So if the Ballets Russes provided the roots of modern dance, the old Russian tradition was kept alive by the dauntless Mrs Inglesby and her elderly mentor. She had to sell the priceless scores to Harvard, as no one in the UK was interested, and The Royal Ballet and even the Kirov itself consulted these papers when the fashion for sumptuous revivals of the classics came back into vogue.

Ever more intellectual: British twentieth-century theatre

Harley Granville-Barker was an English actor-manager, director, producer, critic and playwright. In his productions of Shakespeare's plays at the Savoy Theatre in 1912 and 1914, Granville-Barker did away with the 'star' system of acting and instead concentrated on excellence in the entire ensemble. He directed actors to speak Shakespeare's text rapidly and without exaggerated gestures, and used mainly curtains to create scenery, thus cutting down on the length of performance. He steered clear of elaborate, historically 'accurate' scenery and opted instead for symbolic patterns and shapes on stage, thus setting the fashion in director-led stage productions for years to come.

Michel Saint-Denis (1897–1971) was a French-born actor, stage director and drama theorist whose ideas on actor training had a profound influence on the development of European theatre from the 1930s on. After the Second World War, Saint-Denis founded a new theatre school at the damaged Old Vic theatre in London's Waterloo area that existed from 1947 to 1952, which formed the basis of the National Theatre of Great Britain.

Sir Barry Jackson (1879–1961) was a distinguished theatre director who enjoyed one of the most productive professional relationships of the twentieth century with writer George Bernard Shaw. He was the founder and Governing Director of the Birmingham Repertory Theatre and was also a director of the Royal Opera House in London. He directed the Malvern Summer Festivals from 1929–1937 and was Director of the Shakespeare Memorial Theatre in Stratford-upon-Avon in 1947–48. His 1925 modern dress, or Jazz, production of *Hamlet* for the Birmingham Repertory Theatre caused something of a scandal amongst more traditionalist theatre-goers but was very influential as a directional way of presenting Shakespeare. Michel Saint-Denis and Harley Granville-Barker spearheaded the concept of directors' theatre. Three years later, in 1925, Barry Jackson galvanized Birmingham, and then London, with a production of *Hamlet* in modern dress in which the player-prince was deliberately modelled on Edward, Prince of Wales, whose determination to shake off the fustian image of monarchy struck a chord at the time. In a sense, this was Shakespeare come full circle.

Hollywood

Nobody's designs more fully embodied the spirit of Hollywood fantasy than Adrian (Adrian Greenberg, 1903–59), who obeyed to the letter Cecil B. DeMille's instruction: 'Don't design anything you could possible buy in a store.' Hollywood's costume designers had two main strands: full-on glamour for the romantic leads and modified social realism for almost everyone else.

Opposite Colin Keith-Johnston playing Hamlet. This production was directed by H.K. Ayliff and started in London before moving to Birmingham in 1925.

1940s and 1950s

When the Second World War ended in 1945, despite the joy that the seven years of bloodshed and rationing were over, ordinary life was still fairly colourless and bleak. People didn't want to go to the theatre or the opera and be obliged to sit through more squalor or nastiness. Not surprisingly most audiences wanted an evening of charming escapism, and why not? However as soon as it was possible to move on, the English Stage Company at the Royal Court Theatre did so with the bold concept of a left wing 'writers' theatre'. The company made a real effort to offer an aesthetic far removed from the prettily costumed 'drawing room comedies' and escapist musicals that dominated the West End stages of post-war Britain in the later 1940s and 1950s. Designers such as Cecil Beaton, Oliver Messel and Leslie Hurry mostly worked in London's West End or on the grander opera and ballet stages, and though their work was much loved by audiences, (as it still is) – it could hardly be classed as modern or in any way revolutionary.

This page Sketches of a family wedding party show typical clothing from the 1940s and 1950s. Note the New Look suit above right.

1960s and 1970s

Theatre design as we know it today sprang out of a denial of this decorative painterly tradition, and has its origins in the work of Bertolt Brecht and the Berliner Ensemble, which was first seen in England with a bleak production of *Coriolanus* in the 1960s.

A 1971 production at Stratford-on-Avon signposted the next (some would say other) main direction in costume design. For *A Midsummer Night's Dream*, Peter Brook and designer Sally Jacobs devised a plain white box to create the perfect neutral space for the action, into which the fairies descended on trapezes wearing clown suits in primary colours – not a wig or a corset in sight.

Above *Look Back in Anger*, an example of 'kitchen sink' drama, performed at the Royal Court in 1965.

At the Royal Court Theatre in London, John Gunter and I, working with the director Peter Gill, unwittingly started a style of heightened poetic realism dismissively referred to as the 'Hovis ad school of design'. I might point out that the makers of this worthy brown bread copied us, rather than the other way around.

Costume dramas

In that era of very different values, the BBC was an integrated studio environment with a properly funded costume design department and wardrobe, from which came a stream of lovingly realized costume dramas, epitomized by the sumptuously accurate clothes created in 1974 for Anthony Trollope's epic novel *The Pallisers*. Almost for the first time in the history of popular drama, the costume designer Raymond Hughes succeeded in taking a completely fresh look at the nineteenth-

Opposite *Coriolanus*, performed by the Berliner Ensemble in 1964.

Above A party scene from *Don Giovanni*, with the cast in glamorous 1940s attire.

Right Costume design from *La Belle Vivette*.

century world without feeling the need to stylize it for a contemporary audience. Since then, what might be called classic costume design has become somewhat marginalized, at least in the straight theatre, but has survived in big musicals and on film, for flamboyant period costumes are always popular with audiences, whatever avant-garde directors and critics might say.

1980s to the millennium

At the beginning of the 1980s, the hopeful liberalism that had characterized the previous two decades disappeared and was replaced by a far less attractive stereotype. Modern fashion writers are often rude about the floaty styles of the 1970s, but to a costume designer the less urban manifestations of the style hold great charm. All that craft-revival patchwork and macrame can give a very distinctive look to quite a varied range of productions. And whatever happened to the wildly original designers such as Yakamoto and Matsuda? I could use their strange 'bag-lady' creations as a point of departure for many a play set in ancient times. But the well documented swing to the right, headed by Thatcher in the UK and Reagan in the US began in earnest, and there was no longer a place for charm or whimsy.

Broadway

In New York, musicals dominated the stages of Broadway, with costumes designed in the commercial style of cartoon-heightened realism still common today. It is sometimes argued that while British theatre is literary in origin, US theatre's origins are musical. The coming of colour film combined with the 'can do' energy of performers such as Gene Kelly, James Cagney, Judy Garland and Ethel Merman projected US entertainment across the world.

US theatre continues to evolve. Julie Taymor, working on *The Lion King* (1997), has introduced large-scale puppetry and a cohesive simplicity rich with surface detail in both sets and costumes. Taymor's work has typically drawn on diverse cultural aesthetics, melding inspirations from Japan, India and Indonesia with forms from Chinese opera and the commedia dell'arte.

Costume dramas for film and TV

Right The *Lord of the Rings* trilogy provided some excellent fantasy design.

Opposite Tilda Swinton wears icy blue to startling effect in *The Chronicles of Narnia: The Lion The Witch and The Wardrobe.*

The appetite for accurate and beautifully dressed period dramas, particularly in film and TV, seems insatiable. It doesn't seem to matter if the script is from the past, as in Shakespeare or Jane Austen, or new: think of the resounding success of *Downton Abbey* (2010 onwards) on both sides of the Atlantic. Costume dramas are almost always subjected to a sneering air of condescension by many critics, but the public chooses to ignore such a dampening viewpoint, I'm pleased to say.

Fantasy

From the grittiness of the *Alien* series (1986–97) to *Star Wars* (1977 onwards), the dark extravaganza that is *Lord of the Rings* (2001–3), and the eccentric Britishness of the *Harry Potter* films (2001–11), exotic worlds created by costume and set designers are the defining features of the fantasy/science-fiction movie. The reason for the popularity of such escapism hardly matters. In these difficult times, such films feed a real need: however grim the situation in the world, on screen at least Good will finally triumph over Evil.

PART 2

The design process

HOW DO YOU DO IT?

One of the questions I am frequently asked at parties is 'How do you actually design costumes?' In fact, trying to define the design process on paper is a bit like trying to teach someone to ride a bicycle by letter – everything really depends on the specific conditions and moment-by-moment balance within the situation. The methods have to differ according to the project. Although many of the actual design and making processes are broadly similar, the administration of film, theatre and operas means that each demands significantly different approaches.

Timescale

In opera, the creative team of director and designer(s) is frequently engaged two to three years in advance; for theatre, two to twelve months in advance is fairly standard (longer for subsidized shows, shorter for commercial and fringe shows). However, in film it is not unheard of to get a job on a Friday and start work the following Monday. This is not in itself an issue, provided that you can synchronize your own financial cycle with your chosen medium.

The problems arise when trying to mix stage and film work, since if you're working in the former, you're bound to be contracted in advance; if an agent then phones with the film offer of a lifetime, you're faced with the choice of terminally offending either your theatre director or your bank manager. The other principal difference is that it is possible to work on two stage productions simultaneously (three at a pinch, if they are not too big, or too geographically distant), but film demands thirteen-hour days for six days a week. This is the main reason why so few designers succeed in maintaining careers in both film and theatre, even if they want to.

Above Designs for Hero's wedding dress in the 2011 production of *Much Ado About Nothing* at The Old Globe, San Diego.

Discussions with the director

When the script, text or libretto arrives, read it as carefully as possible. Get the director to take you to lunch, and discuss your initial response (this bit can be done electronically these days, but it's not so much fun). Find out what the director thinks – better still, find out how the director thinks – as your ability to anticipate changes of mind will save much heartache and bad

temper later on (Olympic-level second-guessing, I suppose). Then read the script again, this time making notes. There are as many methods of approaching the design of a set of costumes for the stage as there are productions. It is useful to explore several contrasting design concepts in your discussions with the director – if only to clarify the director's mind by agreeing how you don't want the production to look.

Above Timothy Spall, Sir Nigel Hawthorne and Joan Collins in period costume for the film *The Clandestine Marriage*.

Planning

You need to list all the characters, with basic indications as to relationships and approximate ages – it's surprising how many scripts don't come with a sensible cast list. Find out the number of extras or chorus that you will have to dress, if you can. Work out roughly how many costume changes you would like each character to have in an ideal world, but also how few you could manage with if the budget is small. Find out what the costume budget is, and what it's supposed to pay for. In some companies, staff labour is 'below the line' and only fabric, outworkers and overtime is charged to your budget, whereas with others absolutely everything is 'above the line', including postage and taxis. As the saying goes, 'You can have it brilliant, cheap and quick – pick any two.'

Knowing how much money and time you have will influence both the style and the techniques you choose to work in. For instance, it would be foolish to aim for tie-dyed, hand-printed and embroidered costumes accessorized with custom-made jewellery if everything has to

be ready in a fortnight, whereas if you have only a modest budget but three months' preparation, then cheap fabric, beautifully processed, could be a rewarding option.

Creative satisfaction

It is worth remarking that, despite all the drawbacks and budgetary limitations of the stage, a costume designer is likely to be able to realize her/his design vision much more completely and satisfyingly in the theatre or opera than on most films (except fantasy films on huge budgets), for two reasons. Firstly it is taken for granted that on the stage many of the costumes will be made from scratch, and secondly because all the actors are necessarily present during that wonderful thing called the rehearsal period, the costumes can be properly fitted on their bodies – neither of which is necessarily true of film. I remember a particularly stressful TV costume drama set in the 1820s and 1830s, where 41 of the 50 speaking parts had been forbidden to sign their contracts by their respective agents until the week before it was due to start … and there was almost nothing smart in the rental shops in the relevant period.

Left Curtain call with the cast and creative team at the 2011 production of *Don Giovanni* – spot the designer!

Research

After all this theorizing, it is something of a relief to move into practical mode. I usually try to find paintings or photographs and will perhaps draw a few pencil sketches at this stage, in order express my evolving responses to the text. It is vital not to leave too long between meetings with the director and/or set designer, or your initial ideas may become too fixed to be easily changed. I would expect to be able to pinpoint the kind of costumes needed by the second meeting, also to exchange general ideas about colour with the set designer. This is also the right moment for a detailed discussion about the characters and casting, so that everyone is thinking along the same lines.

With the broad scheme in place, I would now do any further research that might be required. I use a wide range of visual material: paintings, sculpture, photographs, bits of fabric and pottery are all useful, as are magazines and catalogues. One needs to think laterally in identifying sources: there really is no substitute for an enquiring mind! You need to relate whatever you're doing to your wider social knowledge.

Traditional sources versus the Internet

When I first started to make notes for an essay on research back in the 1990s, books, photos and art galleries were the main (no, the only) source of information. Seems a bit quaint now! Writing this in 2013 confirms that the time before the World Wide Web really was another age, because the Internet

Opposite An outtake from the TV series *The Edwardian Country House.* Costumes were inspired by photographs such as the example shown right.

Right A photograph showing an Edwardian woman and man in hunting attire.

has changed everything. Wikipedia, Google Images, Pinterest and enthusiastic personal blogs in Wordpress and the like mean that you can find pictures of anything you can imagine and far more besides. The only difficulty with these blizzards of information is that unless you have some knowledge of the main framework of the development of fashion shapes, you will be unable to select relevant images. There is still an important place for books of paintings, photographs and dress patterns. Indeed, many of us develop quite a serious book habit over the years, as groaning shelves will testify.

The main encyclopedias of fashion history, as you might expect, are a good place to start. They never have enough illustrations of the period you actually want, but their grasp of the main events, both social and sartorial, makes them an invaluable point of departure. I happily admit to making Michael and Ariane Batterberry's *Fashion: The Mirror of History* my first port of call on many occasions, not because the pictures are better than others but because the gossipy text is so lucid about everything, from the sexual preferences of monarchs to the appalling working conditions of Victorian seamstresses.

It is also worth studying the portraits and genre paintings of the time, though not all are equally suitable for costume reference. The attitude and ideals of the artist are often too insistent to be helpful. While Tissot recorded the endless frills of the 1870s with a meticulous idealism that has reduced many a designer to despair, it comes as a surprise to find, on closer examination, that behind Sargent's flamboyant grandeur, the ladies' dresses are so simply stated as to be effectively useless as a guide to the period – a shame, for he is almost my favourite portrait painter.

The flattering confections of the society portrait painters are at their most helpful if the project demands a design concept with a bit of a twist, rather than dramatic realism. For instance, Winterhalter's meltingly sensual paintings provided the perfect point of departure for the 1994 production of *A Month in the Country*, in which Helen Mirren played the beautiful, bored, self-dramatizing heroine.

Above Helen Mirren and Joseph Fiennes in *A Month in the Country*.

Opposite Winterhalter's portrait of Elisabeth of Bohemia provided inspiration for Mirren's costume.

Antique costume

Finally, it is always worth going to look at the real thing. There are good examples of antique dress at the Victoria and Albert Museum in London, the Costume Museum in Bath, and at Platt Hall in Manchester; in the US, there are the superb museums of the Jamestown Settlement in Williamsburg, VA.

Hire companies such as Angels (Morris Angel & Son) and Cosprop in the UK and Western Costume in America also have many originals, but genuine vintage garments are seldom usable now as they're usually far too small for today's actors and the fabric has become too fragile. However, they can be copied or used as a source of ideas or for understanding their construction. You can get away with it sometimes in film, but few antique garments other than shawls or men's clothing will withstand the rigours of a theatre season, and they are so rare now that it seems like a sort of vandalism to destroy them.

Re-enactment costume

It has been said that if you can't find inspiration everywhere, then you aren't looking properly. Sometimes ideas come from unexpected sources. One designer/director I know waits until he has dreamt his scheme, which gives his ideas considerable authority, but the workshops can get very twitchy if the said dream doesn't appear on time. I don't decry this at all: many dreams dredge up buried half-memories that might be useful, as well as creating an image of how you might proceed. My own muse can be a bit dilatory in this regard, but the best ideas do often pop into your head unbidden if you have prepared the mental ground for them.

Another source of both information and actual garments are the various sites and catalogues for the re-enactment community. One of the most useful and informative is Jas. Townsend & Son of Indiana, US, which specializes in the eighteenth and early nineteenth centuries. This firm not only stocks an extensive range of semi-bespoke costumes, but has all sorts of handmade artefacts and costume props such as steel-framed spectacles, watches, writing equipment, shaving and smoking accessories and much more.

If your needs concern an earlier or more fantastical time frame, try companies such as Re-enactment Supplies or The Knight Shop, both in the UK, who can make medieval plate armour as well as bucket boots, clothing and weaponry. If you are after American Civil War supplies, Fall Creek Suttlery of Lebanon, Indiana will be happy to help. I explore this area further in the sources and resources sections.

Left and Opposite Designs for the 2007 production of *Oliver!* at Tivoli Gardens, Copenhagen.

THE FOUR STRANDS OF COSTUME DESIGN

Above A production of *Così fan tutte* at the Opera de Lyon in 2011, staged in modern day dress.

Opposite above Costume deisgn using modern-day dress and chairty shop finds.

Styles in costume design, whether for stage or screen, tend to follow four distinct strands. Each is capable of a multitude of variations, but in the end most schemes fall into one of the following:

• Contemporary clothes

• Period costume

• Post-modern costumes

• Showbiz glitz

Contemporary clothes

Perhaps the most obvious decision is to set a piece in the present – this style of costuming aims to be as close as possible to street or couture fashion (depending on the status of the characters) and seeks to interact with the cutting edge of fashion, similar to the way in which Hollywood once cultivated leading couturiers such as Givenchy to design for stars such as Audrey Hepburn.

Contemporary stage and TV drama generally aims for much broader viewer identification by buying middle-market clothing directly off the peg. (These are known as 'shopping shows', for obvious reasons.) This is especially true of TV soaps, dramas with an element of documentary about them, or any production where the actors are intended to look like ordinary people in the everyday world.

'Kitchen sink' dramas or productions dealing with poorer folk can be sourced from charity shops, catalogues and chain stores. It is harder to make this style work than you might think, so that the end result is a coherent and pleasing image rather than looking like the contents of a Salvation Army shop.

Considering the enormous range of street clothing available, from designer labels at one end of the spectrum to charity shop chic at the other, there really is no need for modern dress productions to be dull. An excellent example of the intelligent use of contemporary clothes was Jonathan Miller's production of Mozart's *Così fan tutte* at the Royal Opera House in 1995.

Colour scheme

A strong colour scheme is very important when using modern clothes, if the overall effect is not to look untidy. There is a good example from Peter Brooke's 'Theatre of Cruelty' days, where he and the designer became so frustrated by the incoherent costume scheme that eventually the cast were told to turn up for the final rehearsal in their own clothes – anything as long as it was red! It looked wonderful. Although these garments were purchased from the actors so that they didn't get left at home, it was still a very inexpensive solution.

It sometimes feels as if colour is the only element that is under a designer's control, since it can seem as if everyone in the building has an opinion and is only too ready to share it. Of course this can sometimes be helpful, but might well be counter-productive. One can also get heavily tangled up in an actor's personal fashion statements. The fact that it is possible to go out to the nearest shopping centre for a replacement is both good – and bad – news. At least with clothes that have to be specially made, the designer has the tactical advantage that everyone else is inhibited from complaining by the considerable difficulties attached to producing an alternative.

Small budgets

Unless you are costuming the latest Bond movie, and need to commission seventeen exact doubles of every Savile Row suit, it is undoubtedly easier to keep within a small budget if you use clothes from the last ten years or so. Charity shops, vintage clothing stores, 'nearly new' shops and dress agencies are all good hunting grounds if the budget won't stretch to designer outlets. Some fashion designers will allow you to buy from their sample collections at wholesale prices, though it can be quite a time-consuming process getting permission and visiting the showroom, only to find that your production is placed in a different season to that of the available stock, and a garment is only available in a size 6.

Right Designs for *Così fan tutte*, with the cast dressed in simple jersey tops and beach sarongs.

Period costume

Perhaps this second strand is what most people think of as 'proper costume'. It ranges from the hyper-historical, museum-ready approach of some film and TV 'costume dramas', to films or plays exploring historical subjects, to the rather looser operatic tradition.

From the middle of the nineteenth century until fairly recently, period plays and operas were nearly always dressed in costumes that reflected the date of the work's composition. This has a great deal to recommend it. Most importantly, the social world of the story is brought to life in a way that helps the audience's understanding of the behaviour and emotions of the characters. Period costumes can create images of real beauty and grandeur in a way that often eludes contemporary dress.

There are many projects where it would seem that nothing but the costumes of the era will do. The plays of Oscar Wilde and Chekhov come to mind, as do modern plays such as Alan Bennett's *Madness of George III* and Peter Shaffer's *Amadeus*, or those Restoration comedies where the language seems more period-specific than Shakespeare. Other ages had different aesthetic values, unfamiliar ideals of beauty and (to us) peculiar ideas about what was sexy, and properly thought-through period costumes can express this like nothing else.

Reflecting personality and class

I make no secret of my fondness for evocative historical costume: I like to understand what's behind people's behaviour, and visualizing them in their own surroundings is one of the ways in which I get inside who they were and why they behave as they do.

I can claim to have made a modest contribution to this genre with my designs for D.H. Lawrence's trilogy of plays at the Royal Court in 1967 (my first London engagement). At that time, accurately observed working-class clothes had never been reproduced on the stage, and the production by Peter Gill was a revelation that was widely copied both in the UK and overseas.

Left *The Madness of King George III* at The Old Globe Theatre, San Diego. The king is restored to health in the finale.

Right Costume design for the character of Fitzroy in the same play.

As that strand of drama gathered pace in the 1970s, I watched with some dismay as many subsequent designers seemed to think that merely copying from original sources was enough to give an organic unity to costumes, when it can never be more than a starting point.

Shapes and simplification

I now feel that having spent so many years studying the underlying shapes of each period, I have acquired a discipline that allows me to interpret them with much greater freedom and is laced, I hope, with humour.

Right Desmond Barritt plays Malvolio in the 1994 production of *Twelfth Night*.

When I did the costumes for the 1994 production of *Twelfth Night* at the RSC, Ian Judge wanted it to be quite clear that Illyria was not some remote fantasy island but an idealized version of somewhere within Shakespeare's direct experience, i.e. New Place, Stratford-upon-Avon at the very specific period of January 1607. Audiences thought that the costumes were entirely realistic, but in fact the only ones that approached the over-decorated embellishment of actual early Jacobean costume were those of silly, deluded Sir Andrew Aguecheek, and the pluderhosen worn by Malvolio, with his yellow stockings and cross-garters. This is one of those instances where the real thing looks so mad, so over the top, that it is perhaps best reserved for making a particular, usually comedic, point.

An approach that I find often works is to take the shape of the appropriate period style and strip it of all decoration. This presents the essence of the period in question through the use of pure shape, without the eye being distracted by any unnecessary detail. This treatment, the results of which are often very elegant, works beautifully for the grander operas, as well as for many plays. Once the designer is freed from the constraints of direct copying, she can invent a simplified costume style, adding such garments as kaftans, long greatcoats and flowing robes for an air of noble grandeur; or head-wraps and pinafore aprons for a more homely look.

Changing the period

Another approach is to use more or less accurate period fashion, but not the period of the story. A good example was the costume scheme for Ian Judge's production of Gounod's *Faust* at the ENO in 1985. We changed the action from the late Middle Ages to the mid-nineteenth century. It was very effective because it helped focus attention on the psychological truth of the narrative. Gone were men in red tights and silly hats; gone also were Marguerite's long, unnaturally yellow plaits and puffed sleeves. Instead, Valentin and the soldiers wore dark French military dress uniforms, while the unsympathetic chorus threatened poor deluded Marguerite in rigid

bourgeois black. Mephistopheles became a dangerously attractive Svengali figure, and instead of a prison cell, the final act was set in a white-tiled asylum with the inmates appearing in the same decayed white, wigs and all, as if they had just crawled from under a stone. The genuine gain in dramatic truth is attested by the fact that this production continued to be reproduced all over the world for more than fifteen years.

Double period costume

The difficult but very effective device of using what could be called a 'double period costume' can also be considered. It is an effective way of tackling a type of play or opera that crops up regularly in the popular repertoire. The works are written in one period, using the language, social conventions and musical forms of that era, but are set in an earlier, usually far more primitive time. *Macbeth* and *King Lear* are classic examples of this genre, as are many romantic operas. Somehow early Celtic plaids and pigtails do not adequately support the refinement of Elizabethan language, or the lushness of nineteenth-century orchestration, any more than plate ruffs or Victorian frock coats quite fit the wild grandeur of the ancient world.

Sometimes, as for Ibsen's early play *The Pretenders* at the RSC in 1991, I have invented costumes that were set in the period of the story but filtered through the eyes of the period of composition. One example was the use of bikers' leathers with ethnic plaids for the Barbarians in Verdi's *Attila* at English National Opera North in 1990: black for the burly chorus, and red with stencilled tattoos for the wonderful bass, John Tomlinson. There is nothing like leather and biker boots to make a performer feel, and therefore look, sexy!

In 2010, the director Adrian Noble wanted to set his production of Shakespeare's *King Lear* in the same time frame as Alan Bennett's play *The Madness of George III* (Noble's other play of the season in San Diego), which was about events in the 1780s. His rationale for this was that the political situation was not dissimilar – that of a deranged king disposing of his hereditary kingdom. The concept was further complicated by the fact that Adrian wanted the play to end up in a far bleaker, more modern period that he called 'Beckett land'.

The solution for me was to draw stripped leather coats for the men and plain, corseted silk dresses for Lear's daughters, all in autumnal shades to echo the clouds of dead leaves on Ralph Funicello's wooden set. These costumes morphed into semi-uniforms reminiscent of the First World War, via the distressed rags of the central storm-blasted heath scenes. It was thought to be very effective, perhaps due to the subdued colour scheme and simple shapes; no one noticed the apparently illogical time travel!

Above Sisters Goneril and Regan prepare for war in *King Lear*. They wear twentieth-century greatcoats over eighteenth-century dresses.

Post-modern costumes

Many contemporary directors and designers feel that period costumes are by definition fussy, and therefore are both distracting and irrelevant to the stripped-down, non-referential æsthetic of post-modern theatre – old-fashioned in more ways than one. If this is the case with you and your director, a fruitful avenue to explore might be the 'no period', non-specific or 'timeless' style of costume.

This third strand embodies the stylistically and self-consciously modernist (or post-modernist if you will; I've never been entirely sure of the difference) approach where the appearance of the costume is dictated by an intellectual concept. This could be said to have originated with the Ballets Russes. Whereas costume in the first two categories is generally the province of a costume designer, in this third category it is often the work of the set designer who wishes to impose a unified design concept on the whole production.

In England there have been two seminal influences on this school: one was the visit of the Berliner Ensemble to London in 1956, where everything was pared back to the absolute minimum specified by the text. This greatly influenced Jocelyn Herbert, who was effectively the Royal Court Theatre's house designer, and through her a whole generation of designers (myself included, in my more restrained moments).

American minimalism

A more recent infusion in this area, American minimalism, has led to the current taste for depersonalized or deliberately inexpressive use of costume. One of the first things that a designer learns is that everything put on stage, without exception, becomes a focus for the audience, setting up resonances just by virtue of being on a stage. The minute an actor enters a stage area, a performance is created, however naturalistic, and is therefore subject to the scrutiny of the audience. Whether actor or director is even aware of this, whatever is worn is therefore charged with significance and meanings, be they positive or negative and, like it or not, it will belong to its time.

One solution to all this has been to 'de-individualize' costumes. This usually involves the use of a semi-uniform, often based on a simple Mao-style pyjama suit. The theory behind such deliberate non-characterization is that by rendering the costume 'invisible', the focus will rest wholly on the face of the actor speaking the text. And it does …

On a less elevated note, variations on this technique can work very well if your project is under-funded, or if you don't have the money for more than one costume per performer.

Post-modern design

Post-modern design, on the other hand, prefers to emphasize intellectual constructs, parallel experiences and narrative forms; sometimes, it could be said, over-playing detachment and irony at the expense of direct emotional involvement, visual attractiveness and any kind of decorative quality. Realistic period costumes are thought to set up too many uncontrollable resonances, to be too distracting, too dependent on attention-seeking craft skills or just too 'pretty' to be relevant. Though it must be said that few audiences are likely to notice the nuances of costume theory thus displayed.

Showbiz glitz

Above Sketch designs for the 'Shapes', the spirits in *The Tempest*. From the 2012 production at The Old Globe, San Diego.

Opposite Parisian showgirls in glitz and feathers.

There is of course a fourth strand, which is good old-fashioned show business glamour. This is perhaps the aspect of costume which is easiest for audiences to enjoy, and is certainly the most entertaining. It relates not only to carnival fancy dress, pantomime and variety, but also to the glorious costume parades of the Folies Bergère and the long-abandoned tradition of the final walk-down in the grander musicals, often involving ostrich plumes and vertiginously high-heeled shoes. (Music hall style, however, has probably been superseded by the terrific creations of glam rock.)

Costumes in this genre are supposed to create a superb spectacle and have the broadest popular appeal. The whole point is to entertain and give the audience a good time. Here, at last, the answer to the question 'Why did you make them wear that?' is always 'Because I thought it would look good!' What a relief: an outlet at last for the show-off within. Interestingly, this area of costume design does indeed generally dominate the setting, because the costume wearers are either expressing outsize personalities or, in the case of the chorus, creating a whirling stage picture, framing the said personalities.

It's a rare designer who is equally effective at both ends of the costume spectrum and can do careful, self-effacing, distressed clothes for realistic productions of Chekhov and also let rip convincingly with feathers and sequins for a musical. However, it's fun to have the opportunity to do all kinds of work, even though it may be like having half your brain devoted to Armani and half to Versace.

Communicating with the audience

Whichever approach you adopt towards the design concept of a production, there are still some further questions that need to be considered. Unless you're deliberately using the non-descriptive route, an effective costume needs to take a number of things into account:

- Information
- Sexual attraction
- Audibility
- Aesthetics

Information

A good costume 'tells' the audience about the status, relative wealth, age, profession or trade, attractiveness, temper and underlying psychic state of each character in relation to the others.

It's worth remarking that people's fashion sense often fossilizes in their heyday. Older people are frequently seen wearing the same style of clothing as was fashionable 30 or 40 years earlier. Queen Mary, wife of George V, wore the same toques, the same long Edwardian skirts, and sported the same magnificent 'mono-bosom' from about 1890 until the day she ceased her regal kleptomania once and for all in 1953. This can be a helpful quality in a costume; even today, when fashions change more quickly than they did in times gone by, it helps to indicate the age of a character by showing how 'up to date' their clothes are. The over-50s will seldom wear miniskirts unless they are deliberately hanging on to their youth. That having been said, in these surgically enhanced days, the rules about suitability are not as rigid as they were even 50 years ago.

Sexual attraction

A costume can help project the relative sexiness (or otherwise) of characters. It is absolutely crucial to get this bit right, given that relationships are the main subject of many plays. The audience must really understand why most of the characters want to go to bed with 'A' but wish to avoid having anything carnal to do with poor 'B'.

This page 'Portrait' costume sketches for the chorus in Puccini's *The Girl of the Golden West*.

There are two main problems to be faced. The first is less than helpful casting. If your consumptive Violetta (from Verdi's *La Traviata*) weighs 100kg (nearly 16 stone) and has a middle rather than a waist, you'll just have to work harder, because the singer still has to go out and persuade everyone that she really is a beautiful dying courtesan. She will not create this illusion if forced into a white crinoline that makes her look as if she is wearing her own duvet. You must find a style that makes her look and feel wonderful.

The second problem is the awkward fact that not all period costume shapes are equally attractive to modern eyes. The rigidly trussed perpendicular styles of the 1580s and the 1880s are good examples of an overpoweringly unflattering dress shape, and are seriously difficult to make look sexy … even though the human race somehow managed to overcome this obstacle to perpetuate itself. Equally unforgiving was the 1930s invention of the Marcel permanent wave, invariably worn with dark red lipstick, which immediately makes the freshest 19-year-old look the same age as her mother. This in itself is a good reason for changing or relaxing the choice of period.

Audibility

Although this is less of an issue in film, a real psychological problem exists on the stage when actors are cluttered with complicated or overly fussy period costume. It is said that this can actually make it more difficult to hear, or at least to concentrate on, an actor's lines.

An effective solution to this problem is to keep the head and neck area as clear as possible when important speeches are on the way – so don't ask Hamlet to soliloquize in a complicated Elizabethan ruff, but clouds of starched organdie might be perfect for silly Osric.

Aesthetics

Every production needs an underlying concept – a stylistic scheme or intellectual world view that defines the overall 'look' of the play. It can be literal, for example *Twelfth Night* takes place in midwinter – January 6, 1607 to be precise – in a chilly country house, with many references to stormy seas and 'the wind, the rain', therefore the concept may be to reflect the weather by the use of fur coats and oilskin sou'westers. On the other hand, the conceptual inspiration might be more metaphysical, taking the line 'And what should I do in Illyria? My brother, he is in Elysium' as a point of departure in the search for a perfect, sunny Illyrian or utopian world. Then again, the impetus may sometimes be as simple as a colour change: for instance the costumes may describe a slow change from the mourning blacks of Olivia's court in the first act to the spring colours of her reawakening to love.

This page Drawings for the 2008 production of *The Merry Widow*, based on the designs of Charles Frederick Worth.

Any number of different ways of treating the same text may be equally valid. Here is Trevor Nunn speaking about his decision to update his film of *Twelfth Night* to the early twentieth century:

Above Trevor Nunn's film adaptation of *Twelfth Night*.

> *We brought it forward to a turn-of-the-century world, for a number of reasons; first because it seemed to me that class was a very important ingredient in the narrative after gender – where a group of aristos take umbrage that a steward who is not of their class should seek to govern their lives, and therefore take their revenge, becoming reckless about it and deciding their cruelty should have no limit. Despite references to Illyria, there's a lot of Englishness, so I wanted to go to a time when those class divisions would be very clear to most people watching – but in a time when all the social detail still made sense. We made Orsino's court into a military academy so that the world Viola came into was one where she really did have to survive as a boy: she had to go riding with the duke, and do fencing practice. And there was quite a lot of comedy in this. But we increased belief in Viola as a boy so there was more of a dividend when all is revealed at the end.*

Shakespeare

Above Petruchio and
Grumio's entrance in *The
Taming of the Shrew*.

Above right and opposite A
drawing for Richard II's gold
leather suit and the same
design in black worn onstage.

I realize that a large percentage of the dramatic examples used have been from the works of Shakespeare. I make no apology for this, partly because every designer working in theatre will chalk up quite a number of his plays over the years and it's helpful to be armed with plenty of concept options. Also, of all the playwrights in the English-speaking world, his plays are perhaps the most 'timeless'.

Of the last ten Shakespeare productions for which I have designed the costumes in the last six years or so, only two have been in a version of Elizabethan fashion: *Much Ado About Nothing* in the open-air theatre at Regent's Park in London in 2009, and *The Taming of the Shrew* for

Above The queens wear outdoor kaftans in *Richard III* performed at The Old Globe, San Diego.

Opposite Different colourways for the mens' suits in *Much Ado About Nothing*.

director Ron Daniels at The Old Globe, San Diego in 2010. The remaining productions include *As You Like It* in the uniforms and pretty puffed sleeves of the 1820s; *King Lear*, in a stark version of the eighteenth century that morphed to the twentieth century; *The Tempest*, where the nobles wore the white tropical uniforms of the Edwardian royal family on holiday; and another *As You Like It*, based on the plump ladies of 1930s artist Stanley Spencer and European refugees from the same period, all at The Old Globe, San Diego between 2010 and 2012.

Finally, there was *Richard III*, in San Diego in 2012, which had a double, if not triple, viewpoint. You couldn't tell whether the soldiers at the beginning were from the sixteenth century or modern times; there were rigidly tailored 1980s metallized leather jackets and tight skirts for the three ferocious queens; rock star leathers for Richard when he decided to upgrade his wardrobe; some eastern kaftans to echo the near East; and the final battle used the modern camouflage uniforms of the Libyan crisis and the death of Colonel Gaddafi. Shakespeare triumphed over all!

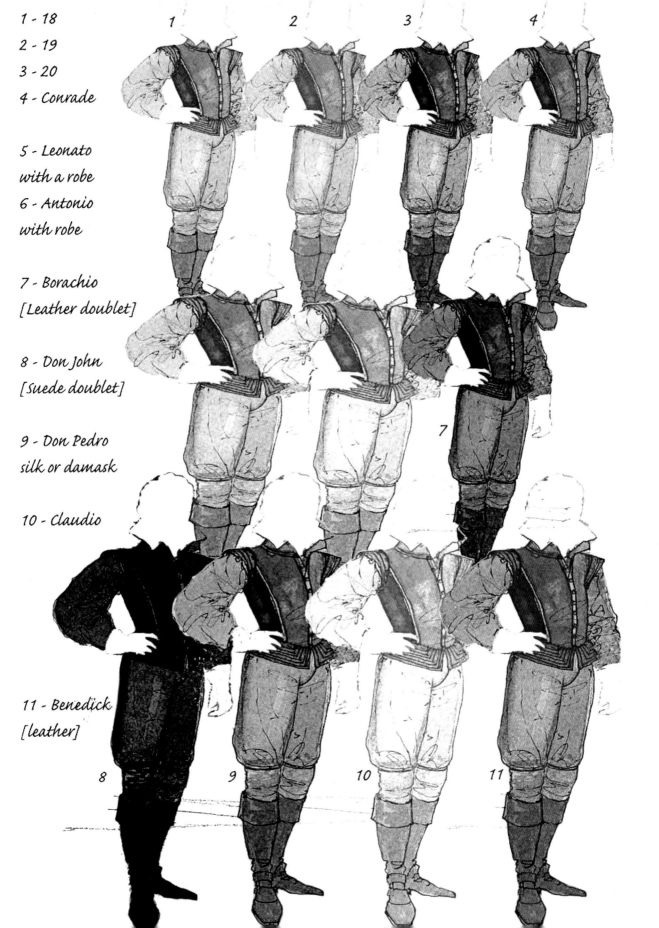

1 - 18

2 - 19

3 - 20

4 - Conrade

5 - Leonato
with a robe

6 - Antonio
with robe

7 - Borachio
[Leather doublet]

8 - Don John
[Suede doublet]

9 - Don Pedro
silk or damask

10 - Claudio

11 - Benedïck
[leather]

Getting it down on paper (and why it helps)

Ever since the introduction of the photocopier (remember those?), students of costume design have been questioning the necessity of making costume drawings, sketches or renderings. And now that so many sophisticated electronic aids are available, it is certainly worth asking if there is still any point in the undoubted challenge that is the execution of the costume design or rendering. To me, trying to express my design ideas for period costumes without clear drawings would be as cumbersome and frustrating as a writer not being able to write. Here are some thoughts on how to make drawing easier.

Left Pencil drawing of the Capulets from the 2004 RSC production of *Romeo and Juliet*.

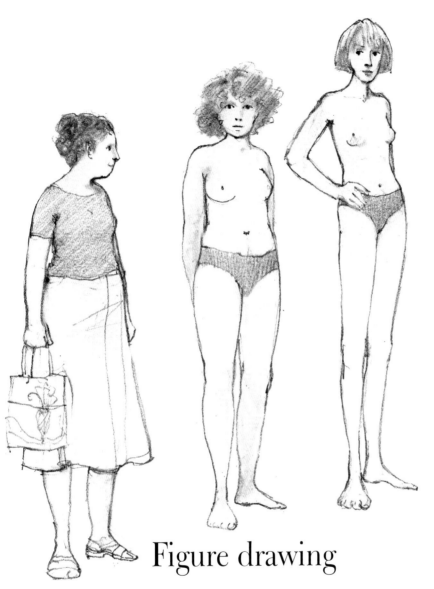

Left My pencil sketches of various body types, which are crucial when designing costume.

Opposite Pencil sketch for the Fool in *King Lear*, with colour notes made with Photoshop.

Figure drawing

Learn to draw the human figure. This might seem obvious, but if you find figure drawing laborious, you will be unlikely to have enough neurons left over to enjoy the actual creative process. The old art school instruction holds good here: keep a sketchbook (and scrapbook) in order to quickly collect a library of different figure types – old, young, fat, thin, sexy, nerdy, and so on. You don't have to do this for ever. Your memory, once trained, will come to your aid, as will the photographic images that you would be wise to collect.

Once you are comfortable sketching all sorts of people, it is a logical business to project these little characters onto a particular period. I call this the Miss Marple school of design, after the Agatha Christie character who was wont to solve her criminal problems when a suspect reminded her of people whom she knew or had seen. It's a simple method of joining character to potential costume design that has never failed me!

If you need to download or make a series of figure templates that you can trace over and use as a point of departure, or use photographs of the performers, nobody need know, and it always charms an actor or singer if the costume rendering looks like their special portrait.

Photoshop and iPad apps

Photoshop is a great help (not to actually draw – I find it too slow); it is very good for indicating differing colourways, thoughts on fabrics and near copies of a basic idea.

One device that is great fun is an app called Sketchbook Pro for iPads. It's quite hard to control for, say, a complex eighteenth-century brocade and lace gown, but charmingly expressive for fairly simple ideas. You can work in layers, as with Photoshop, with the body on layer 1 and the costume itself on layer 2: this means that alterations to one layer leave the rest intact. Also, if you have created a really good figure for a character, you can use it as the basis for several costumes changes.

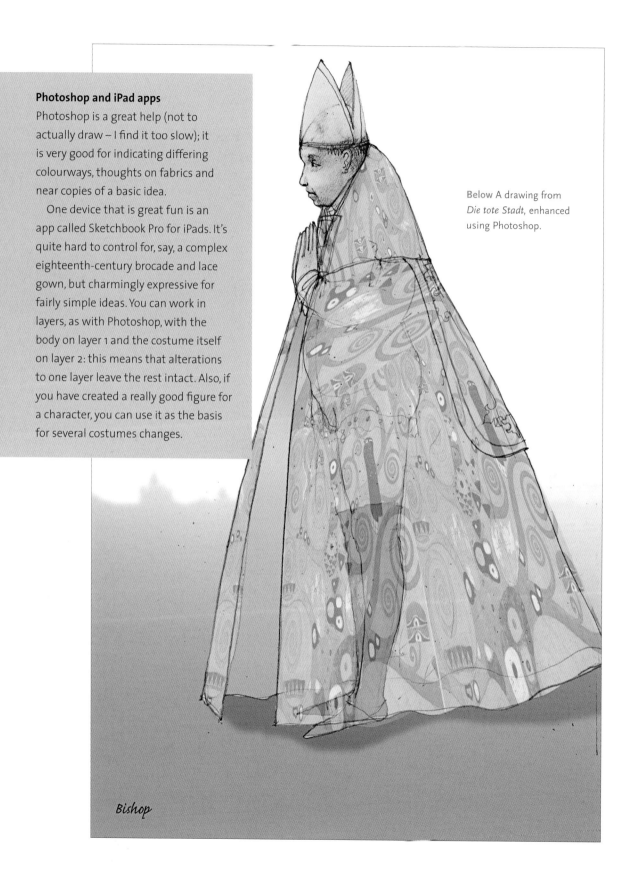

Below A drawing from *Die tote Stadt*, enhanced using Photoshop.

Bishop

Choice of media

Use good paper, matched to the chosen drawing medium. Flimsy paper almost never looks nice. An exception is neatly cut brown kraft paper, which can be lovely with chalks and pen and ink. It's also amazing which types of art paper you can push through your printer: 200–250gsm is fine; 300gsm (my preferred weight to draw on) is about the limit but will go through with a bit of shoving. Tracing paper is actually nice to draw on as it has an attractive 'tooth' that responds well to drawing with a pencil, but if you present drawings on the stuff it is a bit of a giveaway about your methods. However, if you were to scan the sketch into your computer and then print it out on an art paper, it could look very classy.

A rough rule of thumb is to use smooth paper for pencil and crayon drawings, as the marks will smudge nicely. Bumpy watercolour paper is good for water-based paints; choose something somewhere in between for Conté pencil and pastel. Cut all the paper to the same size. Don't make your drawings too big. Few of us draw well enough to maintain graphic interest across paper larger than A3. Huge sketches are such a nuisance to travel with, and how will you fit them into a scanner?

Below *The Tempest*'s Caliban, drawn on an iPad.

Below Audrey from *The Taming of the Shew*. The design inspiration for the costume came from the line 'Bear your body more seemly, Audrey'.

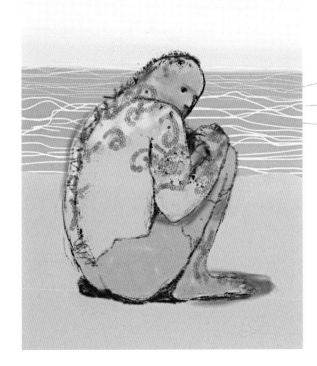

Sharing your ideas

Costume drawings are basically working drawings with ideas above their station. It's enormously helpful if images that are attractive and characterful in their own right can be shown to everyone so that the designer can share thoughts with the director and the actors, but it is worth remembering that their overriding purpose is to impart information. So drawings obscured by complex backgrounds or unrealistic proportions are of little help. By all means do them if you have the time, but you will have to do working sketches as well to make intentions clear to your collaborators.

A good costume sketch, if needs be backed up with research images, 'tells' us about the status, relative wealth, age, profession or trade, attractiveness, temper and underlying psychic state of each character in relation to the others.

Above and Opposite
Designer Charlotte Deveaux's mood boards for *Be a Good Litttle Widow* at The Old Globe.

Mood boards and collages

If you are working on a project set during the last 50 years, or one where the majority of the garments used are purchased or hired, there is little point in making elaborate costume drawings. You are unlikely to find exactly what you have drawn in the right size and colour in a store or hire shop, but if you have a master plan of the kind of thing you are looking for, you may well find something even better. This is where mood boards hold their own, and may even surpass the traditional single figure on a sheet of white paper (which might be preferable for a more built-from-the-ground-up sort of endeavour). A mood board is a collage of reference pictures with scraps of fabric, useful photos and images of inspiring paintings, perhaps heightened with occasional sketches. Here is what American designer David Reynoso has to say:

Mood boards are a terrific way of representing an overall feel for your costume design. Also referred to as 'inspiration boards', these visual collages are an especially useful tool for projects that might require collecting costumes from rental houses or shopping/styling a modern dress film project or theatrical show. These boards function much in the same way as a Pinterest page does … you are able to compile any visuals that inspire how you will proceed at outfitting your performers. However, unlike a Pinterest page, it's important to be choosy about how many images are on one page. You don't want to overwhelm your viewer with too much visual clutter. Therefore, be selective about only displaying what most effectively conjures what you are trying to achieve.

What I like about using mood boards is that they serve as a perfect jumping-off point in communicating the visual vocabulary that will inspire my designs. On one page I am able to assemble many images that speak to silhouette, colour, time period, time of year, a character's age, and materials involved in their clothing. Though I am actually quite good at drawing and painting costume renderings, I find I lean to mood boards more often than not when presenting to my directors and costume shop staff. One is not universally better than the other so long as I am illustrating clearly what I have in my mind's eye.

Right Mood board collage by David Reynoso.

My friend and colleague Charlotte Deveaux also uses this method of presentation for her modern productions. She says:

Collages and mixed-media presentations are creative and interesting approaches to communicate ideas when designing contemporary costumes. Rather than a pencil-and paper sketch, a less conventional artistic approach such as a collage can communicate ideas and design elements and lends itself well to designing a production requiring contemporary costume. When the costume is not to be built, a designer cannot be too specific in the preliminary stages about the final garment. The design is now dependent upon shopping and pulling (from stock or hire shop) and appropriating from other sources.

A collage can communicate the essence, feel, or vibe of the costume through a clever assemblage of clippings from catalogues, magazines, photographs, fabric swatches, research and drawings. I like to include some visual references to the script and scenery to give a bit of a backstory and ground the costume ideas. There is the opportunity, with collage, to play with extreme cut-out sizes and shapes, backs and fronts, and layering for emphasis. I sometimes blow up text that is relevant, include partial drawings, and always try to infuse some humour when appropriate. Collage and a mixed-media approach can provide a good visual vocabulary to express direction, options, and style of a costume while allowing for surprises and unknown elements to emerge in the design.

PART 3

The world of costume

THE CRAFT OF COSTUMES

Getting costumes from theoretical notions to stage or screen is very definitely a team activity. Every designer needs the support of skilled craftspeople and technicians, who will translate her or his ideas (however presented) into wearable garments, deliver the same to stage or film set and look after them once they are there. There are many job specifications within this framework, which could provide a happy alternative to the actual design position. If you are the kind of perfectionist who really likes 'making things', preferring to concentrate on individual artefacts, working on them from start to finish and getting them exactly right, then costume cutting or making could well appeal.

Dealing with the often muddling business of overviews, directors, difficult or nervous actors and the chivvying of dozens of costumes to the finish line, while not actually getting the chance to make anything much yourself, can be exhilarating for some. Helpful support creatively given by someone imaginative is worth its weight in gold, and will often find its reward in continuous employment (unlike, perhaps, the situation of the nervy freelance designer), because if you're talented, reliable and fun to have around, who wouldn't want you on their team?

Above Matthew Bourne's all-male production of *Swan Lake*.

Workers speak out

We did an informal survey of a couple of dozen salaried and freelance workers in a variety of professions connected with costume and found that nearly all of them experienced a high degree of job satisfaction because they felt they were collaborating with others to produce a result which demanded all their skills and ingenuity. They found particular pleasure in their freedom to interpret designs creatively and took pride in seeing the results on stage and screen. 'I enjoy the new people I meet' was a recurring response. The wardrobe manager of a successful touring theatre company said that the variety and excitement of places visited amply compensated for the long hours and low pay.

Below Judy Garland on set in 1944, with a make-up artist and wardobe mistress.

Downsides

Among downsides quoted was 'Being on your feet for twelve hours in pouring rain' (film wardrobe assistant), 'Costume designers who can't make themselves clear and then blame you for misunderstanding them' (draper/cutter/tailor), 'Not enough sleep when things get hectic' (assistant theatre costume designer), and 'Trying to be nice to an actor who has just spilt coffee on their costume when every available hand is busy just before a dress rehearsal' (costume supervisor). Everybody agreed that the worst part of their job was having to produce a professional result when there wasn't a proper budget, or the production team had created an ungenerous or mistrustful atmosphere. Actually, the low-budget production is viewed as a challenge; it's a nasty atmosphere that is the real killer.

The two most important qualities for working in costume, apart from talent, were judged to be patience and good self-organization. One cutter added 'And the ability to bite your tongue in fittings!', while another pointed out that the atmosphere in a fitting made a tremendous difference to the actor's attitude to the costume. A costume supervisor mentioned that anyone in a responsible position had to be able to interpret a script as well as simply reading it.

We asked people if they ever experience

'life-threatening' periods of unemployment. Most freelancers said they did, but that the rewards outweighed the disadvantages. Some people could put their professional skills to good use elsewhere, and others said they had developed sidelines to tide them over. People who had moved into lecturing or curating said that apart from a secure salary, one advantage of a regular job was that you got weekends to yourself. The earnings in film are much higher, in some cases more than double those in the theatre, but are also much more unpredictable.

Jobs in costume and wardrobe

Here are some options. (There is, by the way, a general presumption that the term 'costume' in a job title applies to costume production, while 'wardrobe' applies to maintenance of existing costumes.)

Above Dressing hair in the wig room.

Above right The dye room at The Old Globe.

Wardrobe director

This is a managerial post, with creative implications. The larger theatres and opera companies have wardrobe directors to manage the whole operation of costume production, with all its departments. For instance, the Royal Opera House's wardrobe department produces costumes for the Royal Ballet as well as the opera. This means that there are four main workrooms: Opera Ladies, Opera Men's Tailoring, Ballet Costumes, and the Tutu Room. There are also departments for the making of hats and jewellery, a dye room, a store of costume props or crafts, the buyers' and supervisors' office (sometimes known as the pattern room), a large stockroom of basic and specialist fabrics, a shoe room and the wardrobe production office.

It is the wardrobe director's job to manage all this, while liaising with the main scheduling department (the dreaded Opera Planning or equivalent, who are never happier than when organizing three or four vast chorus operas in the space of a month). A wardrobe director has to sort out the budgets, engage supervisors and act as a buck-stops-here support system when the incipient megalomania of some half-baked director boils over, upsetting a world-famous soprano who has hysterics, and a designer who, having finally succumbed to a long-threatened nervous breakdown, is discovered weeping helplessly in the stockroom.

Costumier for a hire company

These hard-working souls are the people who work with (and, it must be said, sometimes in spite of) the designers, pulling out garments from the over-stuffed rails and turning them into convincing costumes in the fitting room.

You will work with all kinds of performers, from extras to major movie stars. It has to be the best way of learning about period costume, and a number of good costumiers have used their knowledge to become successful designers in their own right. I have often thought that if you were working in Angels (the main London costume hire company) for six months, you really would meet everyone in the business. It has to be the best place in London for the serious networker, and I'm sure that the same can be said of Western Costume in Hollywood or Tirelli's in Rome.

Wardrobe mistress/master

In this position you are responsible for the maintenance of costumes once they have been delivered to the theatre or film set. If you are one of life's carers, this might appeal to you. You also need to take pride in producing an endless supply of clean, beautifully ironed shirts often in trying circumstances, such as the back of a truck, or the dusty attic of a provincial theatre. A good-natured, competent wardrobe mistress or master is highly valued within the company, and crucial to the running of the shows. She or he will also employ and organize the dressers.

Costume supervisor (theatre)/wardrobe chief (film)

Good supervisors are worth their weight in gold, and the experienced ones are seldom out of work for long. The first films I did were all but ruined as experiences because the supervisors were either unsupportive or obstructive; conversely, frighteningly difficult projects have been rendered positive, even happy events with the help and companionship of good colleagues.

The designer is responsible for producing the design choices of the principal actors, but the supervisor is responsible for more or less everything else. The job suits hyperactive compulsive organizers who never give up until every last sock and its spare is in position. You also need the ability to bond deeply with your designer, becoming friend, partner and confidante.

On films, the wardrobe chief is also responsible for arranging such things as the hire of the wardrobe truck, and fitting and workroom space, as well as organizing crowd fittings. It is often possible to become a designer, using your experience as a supervisor, especially on modern-dress projects, but if you do see supervising as a stepping stone to other things, it is not wise to go on too much about your ambitions while working as one, or you will upset the concentration and fragile ego of your current designer!

Costume or wardrobe assistant

For many, this is the accepted way into the business and yet, one of the best assistants I have ever worked with is a grandmother several times over! This job definition only really exists in film and television, for some reason. In a large-scale theatre, there is more likely to be an assistant supervisor or three, and perhaps more than one buyer/shopper (it's just a matter of terminology). The main qualification, over and above the obvious practical skills, is an unquenchable desire to be helpful, and a willingness to learn. You would be expected to help with buying, stock fittings, 'standing by' on the set, dressing, breaking down (distressing) costumes, making bits and pieces, and generally being useful.

Wardrobe buyer

This is the perfect job for a compulsive shopaholic. The buyer will need to know where to find anything that might be needed, bring back samples for the designer to choose from, and then go and collect it all from the store or shop. You will end up knowing your town better than anyone else in the building, and will be greeted as a long-lost relation in all the most useful shops. On a film, the wardrobe buyer is usually also a costume assistant, moving from one job to another as and when necessary, but if you are interested in props as well as costumes, the art department always employs specialist buyers, as do the larger opera houses. These days, much buying is done over the Internet, so familiarity with the best sites and online suppliers is also involved.

Costume-maker/cutter/tailor

Good cutters and tailors are always in demand, and I know of at least three companies worldwide who are looking for first-class cutters of men's period costume, even as I write. These are excellent occupations for creative and skilled individuals who need to work to the highest

Below left Toile or mock-up for Bianca's wedding dress in *The Taming of the Shrew*.

Below middle and Right Fittings for the character of Bassanio in *The Merchant of Venice*.

possible standards, but who might find a position in the firing line, as inhabited by the costume designer, unappealing.

The main qualification, apart from couture-standard technical skills, is an ability to see through a designer's eyes, so that you can find a way of interpreting her sketches, since not all designers know that much about cutting and, if they've got any sense, will welcome sensitive help to manifest their own designs.

Some makers like to work by themselves in their front rooms, or in rented space in one of the many business parks or warehouses now available. Others work with a partner or employ help as and when they need it, or run large workrooms. Those who prefer the security of a regular wage work for one of the larger opera companies or costume houses, according to temperament.

Hat-maker/jeweller/mask-maker

All the above remarks apply, but the telepathic element is even more important, since the designer is likely to know even less about millinery, jewellery or mask-making than she does about cutting, and her drawings will probably will be scrappier and less informative.

Textile crafts

This is an area that interests me very much. Certain projects, especially ones that are set in the past, before the invention of chemical dyes or artificial fibres, rely heavily on hand-processed fabric. It is fairly unusual to find material that is the right weight, colour and pattern, at a price that you can afford, and often, the patterns that you do find are somehow too small and mechanical (or too large and crude) for the effect you want.

I have been known to process every piece of fabric on certain shows, buying the cloth

Left An actress applies her make-up in the dressing room.

Above Make-up test for Alfred as the Player Queen in Stoppard's *Rosencrantz and Guildenstern are Dead.*

wholesale in a raw state from mills such as Whaley's of Bradford, and dyeing, distressing and printing it before it is cut. Certain chemistry skills are needed if you wish to progress beyond the domestic dye-in-the-washing-machine stage to experiment with resist and discharge, silk screen and stencil, or any combination thereof. A few large, subsidized theatres run a dye room, but nowadays most dyers are freelance, working for film, stage or even the fashion industry according to demand.

Hair, wigs and make-up

In the theatre, the costume designer designs the wigs and the make-up. In film and TV, she can only influence. Many years ago, the two crafts were run by separate (warring) unions and extreme cunning had to be employed to get your ideas across the divide. Nowadays, it's not so tricky to get your voice heard.

If you actually want to work in the wig room or make-up bus, there are a number of ways in. The Appendix (see page 220) lists the courses and apprenticeships available. The basic skills of a make-up artist and/or wig-maker could serve you equally well in fashion or therapeutic cosmetic work, but if you decide that the entertainment business is for you, I suspect that the best way in is through an apprenticeship. Nothing compares with actually doing the work and being hands-on. And with university degrees being so expensive, getting an internship could be a very smart move.

Without question, wigs in particular can make or break a look. Some of my worst moments during technical rehearsals have revolved around unsatisfactory wigs. 'Why is that man wearing a cat on his head?' is a phrase I am unlikely to forget. Conversely, if you get the wig triumphantly right, success is probably assured for the whole costume.

Costume research and conservation

It came as something as a surprise to me to discover just how much interest there is in the academic side of period costume. If you are more interested in antique textiles and museum-quality garments as distinct from the somewhat rougher world of getting performers into frocks, working with one of the costume collections, dealing in vintage clothing, or doing research for designers and social historians may be more appealing.

Teaching

I very much enjoy teaching, but in the UK at least, there is less opportunity for part-time work nowadays. This is a great shame for the students on costume design courses, as it is important for them to come into contact with designers who are actually out there, working. The situation seems to be much healthier in the US, where there are a number of superb postgraduate courses taught by practising designers and makers.

Specialist stage design courses are naturally the main sources of employment for teachers, and will be well known to anyone who is established enough to consider teaching others. That said, many costume technicians do a couple of days' teaching a week – providing a regular income and benefitting the students. (See the Appendix, page 220, for a list of costume courses in the United States and Europe.)

One of the great joys of working in theatres such as the Royal Shakespeare Theatre, Stratford-upon-Avon or The Old Globe theatre in San Diego, is the collection of superbly talented people who work in the production wardrobes or costume shops. There was, and still is, an amazingly dedicated team of cutters, milliners, armourers, dyers and seamstresses who are seemingly able to do anything that a designer can think up, and more besides.

In the UK it is a tragic and unnoticed scandal that the last twenty years has seen the decimation of first-class wardrobe departments at the BBC, the RNT and the ROH, which have been the victims of cost-cutting by accountants. The real long-term disaster is that each of these establishments represents an irreplaceable body of knowledge and a focus for the development of traditional labour-intensive craft skills, which could never be viable as stand-alone business units in a commercial environment, but which are absolutely essential to first-class work in theatre or film.

Is this the life for you?

The response of Philip Prowse, designer and director, and my most valued college tutor, to questions about what proportion of his students became successful designers alarmed me very much at the time: he felt that about one in ten had the talent, but only one in twenty had the temperament to go with it. Even if he was being unduly gloomy, that still leaves a large number of students who may have the problem-solving and artistic skills of a designer but who prefer to concentrate on one thing and do it very well, rather than develop the jack-of-all-trades – some would say 'butterfly mindedness' – approach of the typical designer. I would encourage those people to think laterally. There are plenty of other equally valuable jobs you can do in theatrical costume, and in fact all of them can be done better if you bring a designer's imagination to bear on them.

Temperament

If you're wondering whether you do have the temperament of a costume designer, you might like to try asking yourself the following questions.

- Are you bossy enough? Much of the work consists of making other people, often older or more experienced than you are, work for you.
- Will you be able to deal with half-hearted or uninspired workmanship, and find a way of making it better?

• On the other hand, are you too bossy? Must you have your own way? If flexibility and compromise seem like defeat, then the frustrations of the designer's position of pig in the middle between directors, makers and performers will drive you mad.

Reality bites

Because of a costume designer's position in the production hierarchy, it is a uniquely stressful job. Almost all my friends in the business have a degree of irritable bowel syndrome – that is when they don't have actual stomach ulcers! Unless you are successful enough to go from film to film, or lucky enough to have a percentage stake in a long-running musical, it is not a well-paid profession. Moreover, there is no job security! However admired and successful you might be, many things can conspire to put you out of work at any point: fashion, your pet directors giving up, the economy, budget cuts, or the configuration of the planets – and if you have a mortgage and dependents, it's no joke.

The worry about where your next job is coming from never really goes away for long, and although this can be tolerable, exhilarating even, when you are young, single and child-free, when your account is haemorrhaging money on a daily basis and nothing is coming in to top it up, the emotional stress can be quite terrifying. And God help you if your partner is also freelance and hits a bad patch at the same time!

When teaching, I always feel an obligation to discourage anyone who isn't completely determined to be a designer. But with a little ingenuity, some lateral thought and a bit of reprogramming, such a person could easily become a happy, successful and potentially first-rate cutter, milliner, textile expert or supervisor.

Should I be painting this 'warts and all' picture? I realize that I am sounding negative (and there is always room for really good, committed people), but if I succeed in putting you off, then it wouldn't be the life for you anyway. As a way of life, designing costumes has a number of drawbacks that need to be coolly considered before any irrevocable decisions are made. There are very few female costume designers who have managed to combine a career and children, and fewer still who have managed to continue to cohabit with their children's father. If the uncertainty of such a life does not appeal, or your nerves or health are less than rudely robust, but you love the whole ethos of the costumier's world, well, there are many other options that could be even more satisfying, and rather less angst-ridden.

It's a brilliant job

On the other hand, when it works, it's a great life! I have travelled all over the world to work on many productions with world-class performers and directors. You see the best of any given country if you are part of the working community rather than simply visiting as a tourist. And I'm convinced that you meet the nicest people. It's been immensely satisfying; stressful sometimes, but very rewarding.

Opera is definitely the home of big ideas and bold stage concepts. At the more modest end of the scale, touring chamber productions with two or three singers and a small band give much pleasure to many, but at the other end of the scale, opera is not called grand for nothing.

Major operatic productions

The big operas by nineteenth-century composers such as Verdi or Wagner can demand an orchestra and a mainstream production may top 100 players. The costume designer will have to give thought to the house chorus, the extra chorus, actors and sometimes dancers – a considerable undertaking.

In a way, this is almost the main difference between the so-called 'straight' theatre and opera. The designer working on an opera does all the same things as when working in straight theatre, but with a bigger brush. Most of the major opera houses have an orchestra pit that is 3.6–4.5m (12–15ft) across, so unlike many productions of plays, there is no such thing as a 'close-up'. This isn't to say that the designer can afford to be slapdash on the grounds that the audience won't see the wobbles, but she or he definitely has to think more boldly and work with a more expansive confidence.

Below A production of *The Marriage of Figaro* set in the 1950s.

Designing for opera

Below Designs for Adalgisa and a priestess in Bellini's *Norma*.

Opposite Russian court ladies drawn for a 1990 production of *Prince Igor*.

I love working on operas, finding it a great privilege to have an opportunity to get to learn about great music, and have designed costumes for a wide variety of works, ranging from Purcell's *The Fairy Queen*, which was written in 1692, to Korngold's *Die tote Stadt* (The Dead City), composed in 1920. I've not done many twentieth-century works, but the two genres of spoken theatre and opera seem to have become much closer in appearance than older compositions.

Substantial figures

The old tradition of fat sopranos does need to be laid to rest. However, it is a fact that when God gives someone a huge, beautiful voice, they quite often get a substantial frame to go with it. Something's got to support the great big sound that is needed to top a 120-piece

orchestra. I have often heard designers say that they have problems designing flattering clothes for big people and yes, it can be more challenging. Simple, sweeping shapes without much clutter in the way of frilly bits or fussy patterns will look best. Costumes don't need to be black, but thin-weave fabrics in dark colours are more flattering. Many large women have lovely shoulders, so that can be a point of departure. And a good corset can be a great help in tidying up any bulges.

I did a show when one principal begged for something that would help his tummy, so we got him a 'man girdle' designed for post-liposuction flesh control, which took inches off his middle. Far from winding him up about it, all the men wanted one! If a singer is shorter than his soprano, 'tenor improvers' (aka shoe lifts) can be used. It is also possible to buy built-up shoes and boots where you really can't tell that 5cm (2in) is fake stature. It's not a good idea to let heels get too high, though – tottering is never a good look if you are trying to appear heroic.

Personally, being on the larger side myself, I make it my business to make the seriously well-endowed singer, whether principal or chorus, look her or his best. Though I admit it can sometimes be a real challenge, especially for the nineteenth-century repertoire, which calls for the largest voices. Another test is when you have to make an adult look like a boy.

Chorus

The issue that distinguishes opera from other performance forms is the presence of the chorus. It may seem an obvious thing to say, but 20–80 people milling about makes a difference. This slab of humanity can be the size of a couple of train carriages, and you can't pretend it's not there. In some ways, it's not a bad idea to treat the chorus as a part of the set, maybe using simple colour blocks to make the point. However, in some operas you need a 'personalized' group of people, for example *Eugene Onegin* by Tchaikovsky or Verdi's *A Masked Ball*, where a family party is being depicted, and sticking them all in a colour-coded uniform simply won't do. In other operas, one is often grateful for the opportunity to put the gentlemen's chorus in a tuxedo. If you and your director have decided on setting a production in period, this is where a simplified version of the shape in question is often a good solution; you can leave bodices with waists to those who actually have them.

Below The cast of *Eugene Onegin*.

Opposite The chorus, clad in yellow, for a 1994 production of *Don Quichotte*.

Left A design for the character of
Marietta in *Die tote Stadt*.

Modern dress

Latterly, many operas have been set in more or less modern
dress, which can produce its own problems (the size issue
again). But this can undoubtedly create a sense of immediacy
sometimes lacking in more stately solutions. Of updated period
operas, the Weimar Republic seems to get more than its fair
share of outings, and can be creepily effective. There was a 2012
production of Berlioz's *The Damnation of Faust* by Terry Gilliam
at the English National Opera that made full use of this, with
the chase to Hell conducted on a motorbike against a fast-
rotating silent movie backdrop, and poor Marguerite expiring in
her nightie on a heap of bodies in the gas chamber.

Operetta

The operetta only became a distinct form in the nineteenth century, when the term 'opéra comique' suddenly seemed inadequate. New works that were basically romances with happy endings, and often with spoken sections between the arias, began to be termed 'operettas' – little operas. Major exponents of the form were Jacques Offenbach and Josef Strauss on the Continent, and in Britain, the long-lasting partnership of W. S. Gilbert and Arthur Sullivan, who were the stars of the genre.

Operettas were lighter and shorter than the increasingly dark and hefty 'grand operas' of Wagner, Meyerbeer and Verdi, and demanded a far lighter touch from both performers and designers. Other countries also produced populist folk opera: in Spain it was called 'zarzuela'; the loden-clad Bavarian version was called 'singspiel'.

In the first half of the twentieth century, the terms 'operetta' and 'musical' became quite blurred, one often seeming to morph into the other, but with lighter, more populist music and ever more emphasis on dance.

Designing for operettas and musicals

The traditional Broadway and West End musical demands a special approach. Because the singers wear microphones and dance, they are not opera singers but actors who can dance and sing, which quite definitely makes a difference to their build.

On the whole, audiences are not buying tickets to be made to feel miserable (except of course during *Les Misérables*, which used to be known as 'The Glums', where they positively wallow in it): they are going for a great evening out and want to have a good time. This means that the designer can use more bright colours and add much more gaiety to the costumes. This is often translated as meaning swirly skirts with bright net underskirts for the girls and stretch trousers for the boys (so that they can be made nice and tight without splitting during the dance routines). Even when the subject matter is fairly dark, as in *Carousel* or *West Side Story*, the overall mood is likely to at least begin with flamboyance before tragedy strikes.

Left Count Orlovski's party in
Die Fledermaus, performed by
the Welsh National Opera.

Classical and modern ballet

Opposite and Below
Dancers preparing for
and performing in a
production of *Napoli*
in 2008.

If you get the chance to design the costumes for a traditional ballet such as *Giselle* or *Napoli*, in my opinion you have to approach the project with a somewhat different attitude to that for a more modern enterprise. It's rather like being a concert pianist approaching a well-known concerto: make the liveliest, most truthful interpretation in your power, playing the notes on the page, but perhaps let rip with a personal cadenza.

If, together with the choreographer, you have decided to set *Swan Lake* in a prison camp or *Sleeping Beauty* in Hell's Kitchen, these notes clearly don't apply, but the older ballets definitely have an honoured place in the repertoire of our major companies and they can be very satisfying to work on.

Dressing dancers

Opposite Drawings for
the dancers' costumes
in *Napoli*. They were
produced in four
colourways.

In many ways, dancers are the easiest people in the business to dress: they are usually tiny and their wonderful deportment on stage makes anything they wear look its best. The most important thing for them is to have complete freedom of movement, so the invention of Lycra has made everything much easier in the fitting room.

If the ballet involves the classic shapes of the tutu and its knee-length sister, it is as well to study their construction so that you know what you are doing when offering advice in the fitting

room. Many ballets consist of solos and duets by the principal dancers interspersed with group dances performed by the corps de ballet, who will usually think, dance and look as a single matching unit. Variations of tone and colour are allowed, but the shape is normally uniform.

The great Danish ballet, *Napoli*, is unusual in that apart from small groups of three or four soloists, the chorus is realistically dressed as Neapolitan villagers in very, very bright colours. Another tradition in grand ballets is that of a 'chorus' made up of the more senior (i.e. older) dancers, and sometimes of non-dancing extras, who often stand and sit about in decorative postures being courtiers, villagers or partygoers. These folk can wear long gowns, robes or uncomfortable headdresses, as they only have to promenade in a rhythmic and stately way. I know it sounds a bit silly, but it is somehow magical when everything comes together.

This somewhat prescribed way of working is a small part of the dance spectrum. Many operas, for instance, used to contain ballets, which can give considerable scope for the designer's flights of fancy – the Polovstian Dances from *Prince Igor* are a case in point. In my version, the ballet dancers were rather pretty in Turkish corselets and bias-cut antique pleating, which both dancers and audience loved. But they could have been presented in a far edgier manner, as these women rode to war with their menfolk, and were I to do the opera again, I think I would reflect that with more leather, riding breeches and a generally darker palette.

Modern dance

Modern dance is a very different matter. In 1936, an extraordinary young American dancer called Martha Graham made her defining work, *Chronicle*, which signalled the beginning of a new era in modern dance. Out went the white tutus, little net fairy wings, bum-freezer doublets with alarming jockstraps, and in came the modern world. She has not been called 'the Picasso of dance' for nothing. *Chronicle* brought serious issues to the stage for the general public in a dramatic manner. Influenced by the Wall Street Crash of 1929, the Great Depression that followed, and the Spanish Civil War, it focused on depression and isolation, reflected in the dark nature of both the set and costumes.

The costume style most associated with Graham is the dress that she made her own: made from silky jersey, it clung to the upper body before flaring out into a full circle skirt that moved as if it were made of liquid. Her style had nothing to do with prettiness or conventional good taste, but everything to do with expressiveness and passion. (Watch *Night Journey* on YouTube and you will see what I mean.) Perhaps her greatest gift to dance is that she made anything possible – and permissible. Her example opened the floodgates that freed up the imagination of a generation. So if it is now possible to let your Lycra-infused imagination run riot with dance costumes, Martha was probably the catalyst.

In other words, with modern dance, and modern opera productions too, the creative teams now have more freedom than ever before. We have seen Verdi's *Il Trovatore* with the gypsies as crazy people writhing in a madhouse (no, I didn't understand this one either); Handel's *Theodora* with Theodora and her newly Christianized lover, Didimus, being martyred on gurneys by lethal injection; a dance routine where a ballerina in a rabbit costume lies on the stage and clicks her toes as a soundtrack (Opéra de Lyon); and the wonderful Mathew Bourne's all male *Swan Lake*. Anything is possible if you do it with enough chutzpah.

Above Martha Graham dances in her trademark silk jersey dress.

Opposite Designs for the Village Boys from *Napoli*.

MASKS AND PUPPETS

Above Joey from *War Horse*, and his handlers.

If any art forms could claim to be in the lead in the twenty-first century, it would probably be puppetry and animation. Two of the most successful shows currently running are *The Lion King* and the unstoppable *War Horse*.

History

Marionettes are figures on strings or wires; puppets are worked with rods. Puppetry is believed to have been around for more than 3,000 years. This ancient craft takes many forms, but these all share the process of manipulating inanimate objects to imitate dramatic life forms, and puppetry is used in almost all human societies as entertainment, ceremonially in rituals, and to enliven carnival celebrations. European (especially Sicilian) marionettes, Japanese bunraku puppets, Nepalese shadow puppets, the sadistic glove puppets of Punch and Judy, and in our own time, British television's viciously accurate Spitting Image puppets, Sesame Street from the US and Jim Henson's wonderful Muppets, all work with variations on this ancient art form.

What has this got to do with costume, you may well ask. Well, the line between prop and costume design is very porous, and humanoid puppets need to wear something, as do their operators.

A hobby horse

In *The Taming of the Shrew*, which we did in 2010 at The Old Globe in San Diego with Ron Daniels directing, he wanted crazy Petruchio to make his big entrance on a horse – a big hobby horse, the kind that the performer wears as a sort of hooped skirt with a head and tail. These have been around for a long time and I found interesting sixteenth-century references to such things strutting their stuff as part of English Morris dance troupes.

We made ours out of cane lashed together with leather ties, and dressed it in brightly coloured leather strips, which when assembled, looked (a bit) like the tilting finery worn by chargers in medieval combat. It had strings so that Jonno Roberts, our terrific Petruchio, could manipulate its ears and tail. It was very popular with the audience, even though (or perhaps because) it veered perilously close to the realms of pantomime.

Left Sketches for Petruchio and his hobby horse.

Bunraku puppets

Another happy learning experience with puppets came in 2011 at The Old Globe in San Diego, when Adrian Noble wanted the goddesses that Prospero summons in *The Tempest*, as impressive entertainment for Miranda and Ferdinand, to be puppets. I did some sketches using wires, but they were not very satisfactory; then Rory, the head of props, asked if I knew anything about Japanese bunraku puppets. I did not, but on looking them up on Google, it was immediately clear that they would be perfect.

Right Designs for the three goddesses, enhanced using Photoshop.

Opposite top left The Juno puppet blesses Miranda and Ferdinand.

Opposite top right Rehearsals with the unfinished puppets.

Opposite The puppets in the performance.

These traditional wooden puppets are usually 60–90cm (2–3ft) tall and operated by two skilled people: one for the head and right arm, and one who looks after the body and the left arm. There is sometimes a third operator for the legs. The Old Globe runs a postgraduate acting programme, which meant that the students who were playing the spirits in this production could be taught how to operate them.

I designed the creatures and Rory made the heads from translucent cast resin; jointed wooden arms were fixed on to little T-frames that formed the shoulders and torso handles. They didn't need legs, as flowing robes suggested the rest of the bodies satisfactorily enough. I had drawn stick-up hair, a windblown bluish halo, but all experiments looked dismal until

I remembered the nylon dress stiffener called crin, short for crinoline (or horsehair – because it was once – in the US). It worked brilliantly, and there was a happy day when we all – set designer, production manager and Prospero included – sat in the sun and shredded yards of the stuff to help out.

Everyone loved these little creatures, and when the season was over, two members of the cast had got so good as puppeteers that they both got jobs on the fourteen-month-long US tour of *War Horse*.

Animal costumes and puppets

Julie Taymor's designs for the 1997 Broadway production of *The Lion King* were, of course, of a very different order of magnitude and involved many different crafts. The bright costumes were based on traditional African ceremonial garments topped with animal head masks. These mostly sat on top of the head so that the actors' heads were not obscured, and definitely referenced the Disney cartoon film on which the musical was based. The true puppets were the smaller animals, such as deer and so on.

With the production of *War Horse* at the National Theatre in 2009, the huge puppet horses absolutely took centre stage, with the humans coming a rather poor second. I have given much thought to why good puppets are so effective, so involving and moving. Clearly, the design of them is important, but I think they stand or fall by the 'life' lent to them by their operators. These can be out of sight altogether as with marionettes, almost invisible as in the case of Japanese bunraku (or my *Tempest* goddesses), or clearly the emotional drivers, as in *War Horse*. Dressed in simple brown 1914 work clothes, the operators were brilliant. Audiences wept when the horses seemed to die, as their handlers slowly collapsed inside them, their spirits apparently leaving them. It must be something to do with the triggering of our imaginations, I suppose.

Right The Broadway production of *The Lion King*.

Training

If you want to explore puppet- or marionette-making in depth, courses can be found in such places as Prague and are also run by some puppet theatres in Europe and America. For a fuller list, see the Appendix (page 220). I suspect that an apprenticeship is mandatory as well.

Above Puppeteers operate puppets created by Jim Henson.

Courses also exist for mask-making, although traditional mask-making is often an adjunct of the props department. To reach a high standard, you would probably be advised to go on one of the many courses available on both sides of the Atlantic, where you can practise making anything from traditional Greek or commedia dell'arte creations to the more fantastical inventions of modern adventure films.

A related skill is based around the use of prosthetics, in which a combination of pre-modelled facial or bodily distortions are combined with complicated make-ups involving silicone and rubber preparations. This is a highly specialized craft using specially made life casts; jobs can range from making almost invisible nose extensions to creating oozing cadavers for horror movies.

Above Animal masks for the dance in *Much Ado About Nothing*, made using aluminium mesh, hot glue and gold paint.

There are many occasions when even the modest amounts of money available to a small-scale professional production are out of the question. School plays, performances by amateur opera and dramatic societies, fringe shows and student productions must be completely costumed for perhaps less than the cost of a single principal's costume for somewhere like The Metropolitan Opera in New York or the Royal Opera House in London. When costumes are needed really cheaply, even the major costume hire companies will be out of bounds, since their charges are still too high.

The cheapskate checklist

Here are some points to remember when designing on a tiny budget. The bit about colour applies to larger budgets too, but it is crucial when there isn't much money.

1. Keep the colour scheme strong and simple.
2. If you make costumes, use the minimum of pattern shapes.
3. Don't attempt to use realistic period costume.
4. Don't even consider using wigs.
5. Make sure that you arrange enough help.

Ideally, costumes need three attributes: money, time and talent. And since we know that there isn't any money to speak of, let's consider what can be done with the other two. If you have the time, it is possible to make and decorate all sorts of garments and accessories in an original and imaginative way, which will be far more interesting than costumes that have simply been hired or purchased.

Leadership

In my opinion, it is crucial that one person is in charge: drama creation is absolutely not a democratic art form, and as with directing, you need one person who is clear-sighted, competent and bossy enough to get everything done. If a designer is experienced and wily enough, then it will be her (or him); and if she is seriously clever, she will let her helpers think that solutions are all their idea.

Right *Inherit the Wind*
performed at the The Old
Globe theatre.

Dyes and patterns

If you can count on the services of some clever seamstresses and perhaps someone who is a good colourist, you could consider buying cheap, undyed fabric direct from the mill, processing the material with packets of Dylon's Wash and Dye and fabric paint, and making simply cut costumes out of it. This method, which has the potential of producing costumes of real beauty and originality, is used at all levels, but is of course immensely intensive in terms of time and labour. It is certainly worth considering if you are producing something with an element of fantasy, say for the fairies in *A Midsummer Night's Dream*, or Gilbert and Sullivan's *Iolanthe* for that matter.

If you could find a helpful pattern book, such as the Janet Arnold series, or can contact a good cutter who could work out a simplified period pattern, then even quite difficult costume shapes, such as those of the Restoration, or even the 1890s (for productions such as those of Gilbert and Sullivan or Wilde) can be attempted.

If all this seems far too complicated, another method to consider also involves the use of dye to give a sense of unity to existing garments. To me, rules 1, 2 and 3 of designing a pleasing set of costumes on a tiny budget involve the clever use of colour – the less money you have, the fewer colours should you use for a smart and coherent effect. With Handel's opera *Hercules,* produced at the Buxton festival in 2004, we had enough money to make fairly simple costumes for the principals, but almost nothing was left over for the chorus. I had a number of aims for this group of two dozen assorted singers. Firstly, they should look as if they lived in a hot climate. Secondly, you shouldn't know if they were modern or ancient, or indeed what social class they were, as they were not obviously warriors, court officials or peasants. And finally they should have a certain cool elegance within the mainly black set. I decided that they should all wear a narrow colour range between un-bleached calico and pale sand or stripped pine.

We therefore did a trawl of the local thrift and charity shops and bought all the long white cotton skirts, blouses, waistcoats and chinos we could find, and made up any gaps with simple Indian shirts, Khurtas and cotton pants. We found sandals for everyone, ethnic macramé belts and pale cotton head-wraps for the girls, then held fittings that were basically somewhat retro dress-up sessions. They looked lovely in the end, and no one knew that they had cost next to nothing.

Sourcing garments

The garments used can come from a variety of sources. With skillful selection and processing, your production can have an interesting 'look'. Charity shops, jumble sales and unwanted garments from your group's wardrobes are all possibilities; for the more modern minded, cotton singlets and leggings combined with second-hand greatcoats will give you a fine contemporary grungy look. If postmodern irony is preferred, put the said greatcoat over an old evening dress.

Opposite Costumes from *Inherit the Wind* were sourced from original garments.

Period productions

If funds are very short, the use of conventional period costume is probably best avoided. Everything about pre-1920s costume is expensive. This is mainly because before 1920, clothes were so highly structured. Women's garments nearly always called for the use of a rigidly boned corset and several underskirts, as well as the occasional addition of such delights as bottom pads, bustles and panniers. I feel that unless you have the expertise, the time and the money to get the shape right, it's better not to bother. There are other ways of creating an interesting look without wrestling with steels and whalebone.

Changing the period

It is worth thinking about changing the period of the production to one that is manageable on the budget and the skills that you do have, rather than insisting on sticking to the date of the composition come what may. Many plays will look very good in modern clothes. Many of Shakespeare's plays, for instance, update well, as do most texts that are written in one period but set in another. An effective school production of *Macbeth* that I saw used Army Cadet Corps battledress for the endless soldiers, and dressed the witches as bag ladies. I was tempted to suggest turning Lady Macbeth into a Mrs Thatcher clone, but thought it better not to interfere. Clothes from the last 30 years are fairly easy to find in the better charity shops, and can be made to look very good with a bit of care.

Opposite The Tennessee Williams play *Summer and Smoke*, set in the 1940s.

Below The stars of Baz Lurhmann's *Romeo + Juliet* wore Hawaiian shirts and had tattoos and dyed hair.

Ancient times

Plays and operas set in the far distant past can be much helped by the 'tie-dyed singlet and overcoat' approach. Long ethnic skirts or sarongs, or cotton trousers tucked into boots or worn with sandals, can make a simple and effective look for *King Lear* or *Cymbeline*. After all, no one really knows what ancient Britons, Norse gods or Druids looked like, so why worry?

Mixing periods

The other point to consider is whether all the characters in your production have to be set in the same period. This is not quite such a mad idea as it sounds, especially for a work such as *A Midsummer Night's Dream*. I designed this production once where the humans were dressed as for the nineteenth century, but the fairies were rather like threadbare, ghostly Elizabethans, with spider's web farthingales and thistledown hair. It would have worked just as well with the humans in modern dress and the fairies in crushed Jacobean, or faded, bleached punk, or deconstructed 1970s clothes (i.e. charity shop finds that can be artistically shredded).

High society

The plays and musicals that cause the biggest headache for the impecunious costume designer are those social dramas that deal with high society. Here I would include operettas such as *The Merry Widow*, *The Student Prince*, most of the works of Gilbert and Sullivan, the Restoration dramatists and anything by Oscar Wilde. Wealthy aristocrats having parties are extremely challenging to do convincingly on the cheap.

It is certainly worth considering hiring costumes for such period pieces. Out-of-town hire companies are usually much cheaper than the main ones and often have sets of costumes for popular plays and musicals. Your local theatre may also be able to help. It is sensible to approach them with a fairly open mind. For instance, it is not much use insisting on a set of 1850s crinolines for your production of *La Bohème* if they are already booked for an amateur dramatic performance of *A Christmas Carol*. Look and see which period is well represented and invent a concept to justify it. All those freezing students in *La Bohème* would look every bit as good in 1920s blazers or 1950s moth-eaten sweaters and old trousers.

Opposite Prospero in *The Tempest*, dressed in Indian-inspired linen.

Right A design for Oscar Wilde's play *Salome*.

School productions

School productions are a special issue. It is all too likely that the drama or English teacher will find herself responsible for everything. If you are lucky, there will be some committed parents who can help with sewing, or maybe a couple of really enthusiastic students who will organize things. I don't think you will find many as enterprising as Annalee (see below), who took over her school production to great effect, but it can happen. It is also unlikely that many parents will be able to construct dressmaking patterns themselves unless they are already in the fashion or theatre business, but sewing up simple garments that are pre-cut or at least made from one of the excellent commercial paper patterns now available could well be manageable.

I had a correspondence recently with Annalee, a high school student from Cleveland, Ohio, who was responsible for her choir's production of *Joseph and the Amazing Technicolour Dreamcoat* and wasn't sure where to begin. It may be helpful to see some of the questions she asked and my replies to them.

Annalee (A): I have some questions about colour palette and special effects. How do you make quick adjustments when an actor or actress gains or loses weight right before productions? I usually just rely on safety pins.

Deirdre Clancy (DC): Nothing wrong with safety pins, except they are not very safe if dancing is involved – use a nice belt instead, maybe?

A: Do you take the colour of the backdrops and lighting [into consideration] when designing? What are some tips?

DC: Yes, certainly the background and/or set. You have to think which colours will show up well, express the mood of the show etc. The lighting designer should follow you and the set designer.

A: Which is better, Velcro or snaps?

DC: Snaps if you must; Velcro is stiff and noisy, though it can be very useful for quick changes if desperate. Use hooks or buttons if the garment is fairly fitted. Zips sometimes get irrevocably stuck and are hard to mend in a hurry, so are not used much for period costume, but you shouldn't be needing them in *Joseph*, really.

A: Are the little details worth it when the audience is far way?

DC: It depends what you mean by little details! Unless you are on a huge stage with a 4.5m (15ft) orchestra pit, the folk in the front rows will actually be very close indeed; bad sewing always seems to show.

A: We are on a very low budget; well no, we really don't have any money. So would you focus on the major cast members or the major scenes?

DC: The show is *Joseph*, isn't it? If I were you, I would focus on the main characters (that dreamcoat will take quite a bit of work!) and make the chorus wear their own clothes. But tell them to all wear one colour: red or creamy white always looks good. It will look much smarter that way. Maybe your mother would let you dye a bunch of T-shirts in your washing machine (the dye doesn't stain the machine as long as you do the rinse cycle properly). Preferably no jeans, unless of course your chosen colour is denim blue, and absolutely no logos, unless you have printed T-shirts specially and they are all the same. Make everyone come to a rehearsal with the clothes they intend to wear, so that you can weed out anything that doesn't fit in. If you are going to be a costume designer, you have to be quite bossy!

A: What colours would you not use on stage?

DC: I don't particularly like chemical colours on stage, but that is a matter of taste. If you have a solid chorus and background colour, the principals can be as bright as you like – it's up to you.

A: How do you age a character throughout the play?

DC: Grey hair always helps (you can get whiteish mascara, which works fairly well). Neutral colours and the actor's less upright posture will help.

A: Which materials and styles do you favour on stage and which not?

DC: I'm not fond of polyester: natural materials always seem to look best. Keep the clothes very simple indeed – they will look better.

She told me this was all very helpful and that *Joseph* had been a success for them all!

FANTASY

Whether it is because everyday life in the twenty-first century is so stressful or because of our darkening worries about the economy and the planet, there is little doubt that the fantasy genre is alive and kicking as never before. There is much cross-fertilization between the media with books, comics and computer games all providing rich sources for movies, which in turn are occasionally turned back again into computer games.

Films

Some extremely successful films fall into this category. For example, the *Superman* and *Spiderman* series are based on children's comics, the *Harry Potter* films come from J.K. Rowling's books, *The Golden Compass* comes from Philip Pullman's trilogy, *His Dark Materials*, and *The Lord of the Rings* films from the books by J.R.R. Tolkien. Magic and the concept of other, parallel worlds are at the centre of these stories, and seem to hold an endless fascination for many. Darker stories such as the *Mad Max* series, the *Alien* films and the seriously creepy *Hunger Games* are all set in a dystopian future that is both violent and chilling.

Harry Potter and The Golden Compass both ran into serious difficulties with the American religious right, *Potter* because of its cheerful depiction of witchcraft and wizardry, and *Compass* because of Pullman's perceived hatred of the Catholic Church. Whatever you might think of the originals' moral suitability and world view, such projects offer splendid opportunities for inventive designers, as the creative team does indeed invent the universe, colouring the films in the most profound of ways.

Unlike productions of Shakespeare, no one has ever designed these specific worlds before. Designing for fantasy film is almost the only occasion where true originality is possible. Having said that, it is impossible to design a costume that is totally without roots. Everything you put on a stage or in front of a camera will set up a resonance or remembered reference of some sort, like it or not. It is the skillful controlling of such reminders and resonances, combined with bold invention, which will make the visuals truly memorable.

Left A battle scene from
*The Lord of the Rings:
The Fellowship of the Ring.*

Inspiration

Alien and its accompanying elements were designed by Swiss surrealist H.R. Giger, an artist who must live in a seriously scary place. Who can forget the powerful image of the alien creature itself? The film wouldn't have had anything like its power without this iconic piece of design.

Although a bit on the bleak and violent side for my taste, I am a great admirer of the costumes for the *Mad Max* series (1979 onwards). They are also an excellent example of how to go about creating a complete and logical world. I spotted references to punks, heavy metal rockers, Hell's Angels bikers and the singer Marilyn Manson, all stewed together and pushed out with added leather, dreadlocks, fur and missing sleeves. You have to be brave!

This page Sketched ideas for punk, goth and grunge looks.

Opposite H.R. Giger's alien creation.

Opposite Ballet costume by Jean Bérain with an elaborate feathered headdress.

A few words about feathers

Birds' feathers have been used to adorn the human body for a very long time. The tail feathers of exotic birds have been made into fantastic headdresses ranging from the that of the Aztec ruler Montezuma II to the Native American war bonnet, the strange 'Roman' costumes worn by eighteenth-century *castrati*, Brazilian carnival outfits, English court dress (debutantes had to wear three white feathers in their hair to be presented to the Queen), tragic heroines and the diplomatic service's cockaded bicorn hats.

In most early societies, feathers were only worn by male warriors and gods, for instance in the case of the Native American war bonnet, which was typically made from eagle's feathers. For a young brave to earn a feather, he had to carry out a feat of bravery or danger. It is perhaps ironic that now the use of feathers in a costume is exploited as a different kind of mating display, as in the showgirls' costumes of the Folies Bergère and the nightclubs of Las Vegas.

At the beginning of the twentieth century, society ladies wore enormous feathered hats, sometimes involving entire stuffed birds. Many exotic birds, such as the lyrebird and bird of paradise, were trapped almost to extinction by the insatiable demands of fashion.

Headdresses

The first illustrations of feathered headdresses being worn on the stage seem to be from the seventeenth century. Designers such as Henri Gissey and Jean Bérain produced spectacular ballet costumes based on Roman armour, which were worn with a full-bottomed periwig and a peculiar architectural hat or helmet – and as many ostrich feathers as would fit. Bérain illustrated a female dancer with castanets, wearing a rigidly boned and framed seventeenth-century dress, puffed sleeves, and a wavy coronet with eleven feathers. It's a good thing that baroque dancers were not required to raise their legs much, as their dresses would not have allowed this: the dance style demanded intricate footwork (reminiscent of Irish traditional dancing, as in *Riverdance*) and graceful arm gestures.

Perhaps the showiest costumes of all were the kingly matching horse and rider ensembles for a Louis XIV pageant or horse ballet. One cannot imagine what such a thing would cost today! Not to mention those stocky, dressage-trained horses.

Above The ultimate
cabaret costume.

Cabaret

By the end of the nineteenth century, feathers on stage
had been hijacked by cabaret, and have remained a staple
of showgirl costumes to this day. I believe the rule, when
designing costumes involving towering feathered concoctions,
is that the feathers should be as long and voluminous as
possible, but you have to stop at the exact point where
another inch will cause the whole thing to collapse under its
own weight.

Feathers may be 'feather-light', but a showgirl's headdress
is not as light as all that by the time you factor in the
frame and the wire support; it also has to stand up to the
actual dancing. Her costume must be among the most
uncomfortable ever devised – with heels that are 10cm (4in.)
high, a spangled bra, a sharp-edged G-string or thong, as
many wired ostrich feathers as will fit on the dancer's head,
and for modesty's sake, a huge feathered fan in each hand.

The designing of costumes for cabaret is a highly
specialized craft. It is as much light engineering as costume
design – see the remarks about headdresses. The designer will
need the help of a skilled wire-worker and corsetière.

Working with feathers

When I started work in London during the late 1960s, if you
wanted feathers for your costumes, be it for a showgirl's headdress or a simple hat, you had to go
and see Miss Rule (I've only just realized the possible S&M connotations of that name!).

She was a respectable lady of a certain age who worked with a couple of put-upon assistants
in a shabby attic in London's Soho. There were no other options at the time. You had to visit
her and choose what you wanted from her varied stock and she would steam, wire and curl your
choices while you watched. Now, like everything else, you can buy feathers over the Internet,
which isn't nearly such an adventure.

Looking after feathers takes some care. The hatter at the English National Opera once
offered me some free feathers for a costume from his secret store, but when he opened the box
the contents were moving – crawling with tiny creatures. Ugh!

Pop stars and celebrity stylists

In 1963 the four Beatles were persuaded out of the scruffy black leather bomber jackets they had bought in Hamburg and into grey, collarless suits. And ever since the menswear designer Douglas Millings produced his take on Pierre Cardin's unstructured mohair suits, which gave the band its original uniform look, there have been celebrity stylists. They weren't known by that term to begin with, but striking costumes have long been a very important weapon in the popular musician's arsenal. By the 1970s, the most stylish pop musician of them all in the UK was the androgynous David Bowie.

Bowie's first designer/stylist was Celia Philo, who was responsible for the lightning strike make-up worn with dyed red hair and pale skin, but his longest serving collaborator was the Japanese designer Kansai Yamamoto, who created a thrilling and ever changing series of 'looks' for Bowie. Bowie was also inspired by the photographs of Sukita Masayoshi.

In America, while the original rhinestone cowboy was Elvis Presley, designer Michael Travis was designing ever more outrageous costumes for the glittering pianist and showman known as Liberace. These musicians were well aware of how dependent they were on the visual side of their performance, so much so that Liberace refused to do a radio show because he knew full well that his musicianship was possibly not quite in the same league as his theatricality.

Above A showstopping Liberace covered in pink feathers.

Designing for pop musicians

When designing outfits for performers, it is hardly necessary to point out that the aims are somewhat different to those of straight theatre. You are certainly not even trying to produce a homogenized scheme, for a show costume is supposed to be as flamboyantly individual and sexy as possible.

For the girls, outfits are often based on a figure-defining boned corset. Madonna has appeared in a pink spandex corselet with circle-stitched torpedo breasts, designed by Jean Paul Gaultier, as an actual costume; usually, however, such support is invisible. Both Lady Gaga and Miley Cyrus have worked the nude underwear look. Kylie Minogue's showgirl costumes for a recent tour are a good example of the decorated corset, as is Cher's black net and leather number, which suggested that the singer was actually naked under the straps and wisps of net. Most importantly, a singer's show or video promo outfit has to have a strong idea that expresses the singer's beliefs, orientation or the theme of the album.

Lady Gaga created a global sensation by wearing a now infamous dress made entirely of raw beef – flank steak to be precise – to accept an award in 2010. The dress was designed by Brazilian fashion designer Franc Fernandez and 'styled' by long-time personal stylist Nicola Formichetti. After the hoo-ha had subsided (not surprisingly, vegetarians and animal rights groups didn't see the humour in it), Formichetti landed a prestigious gig revitalizing Diesel, the flagging fashion group. Success, both social and financial, is clearly his.

In 'real life', the top stylist Rachel Zoe of Los Angeles is responsible for the sartorial successes of such Hollywood A-listers as Keira Knightly and Nicole Richie, who seem unable to buy anything without her input.

The stylist, newest job on the block, is clearly a career to be reckoned with.

Becoming a stylist

This is what the British College of Professional Styling has to say:

'You'll find the stylist at work with advertising agencies, magazines, production companies, Internet publishers and advertisers, celebrities, catwalk models, photographers, fashion shows, recording companies, TV shows, commercials, catalogues, editorial work, public appearances, concert performances and music videos. Many more stylists make an excellent living from image consultancy and personal shopping services. Or, food styling and visual merchandising.'

Below The Tokyo-Pop suit worn by David Bowie during his *Aladdin Sane* tour.

And the important summing up:

> *'Stylists know how to create the look, develop the image and identify and interpret current and future fashion trends.'*

Some successful stylists feel that paper qualifications are unhelpful and that the best way in is to seek an internship with an established designer or stylist whose work you admire, and then work your way up by hard work. Helping yourself to some of the said stylist's contacts and clients is probably not unknown either. If you have trained as a theatrical costumier and want to get into fashion, or if you are a fashion designer who yearns for something more theatrical, a career as a stylist might well be of interest.

Left David Bowie on stage during his colourful *Aladdin Sane* period.

PART 4

Practical
period costume

Exploring practical costume

I am not a costume-maker or pattern cutter, so you will need to seek out specialist courses, books and websites to take your knowledge of these crafts to a higher level. Think of this as a gateway book, which will give you ideas and a language that will both inspire you and help you to ask the right questions so that you can, if needed, research more deeply. This section explores the actual process of making a historically aware costume. I may not be able teach you how to construct museum-ready reproductions of any given period, but I will try to show the development of shape through the centuries, and how convincing costumes for performance can be created using this knowledge as a point of departure.

EARLY MEDIEVAL PERIPOD (C.500–1100)

The re-enactment societies are probably the best source of clothes from the early medieval period (or Dark Ages); their care and attention to detail is legendary. These ancient times are seldom demonstrated realistically on stage because such primitive garment styles often look unconvincing, not to mention silly, in the indoor, artificial settings of a modern stage, on well-scrubbed modern actors. Film and television is a different matter, however, with productions such as the *Merlin* series (2008 onwards) and the beautifully designed film *The Name of the Rose* (1986), in which the discomfort, filth and level of physical and mental deformity seems almost too accurate for comfort! *Game of Thrones* (2011 onwards), which although a fantasy is clearly based in some remote past, also looks believable.

Celts, Saxons and Vikings

Recently, many extraordinary finds have come to light in bogs and melting glaciers, including a pre-Viking woollen tunic dating from around 300 BC made from brownish woollen cloth; it's strangely touching to think about something so intimate from so very long ago. Other sites have yielded remarkably well-preserved clothing: that of Bocksten Man, for instance, and a complete winter set of clothes from the Kragelund Bog, much later at 1040.

I especially like the tunic worn by Bernuthsfeld Man, who was discovered on 24 May 1907 when peat workers unearthed his skeleton and clothing. His heavily worn tunic was patched out of 45 single pieces of cloth, in twenty different fabrics in nine different weaving patterns. Looms were very narrow, sometimes only 23cm (9in) wide, so a costume scheme for this period that used patchwork would be a beautiful, if labour-intensive, way to go.

If you can find a copy of Max Tilke's book of ethnic and global costume drawings and diagrams, *Costume Patterns and Designs*, he will tell you everything you need to know about ancient and ethnic garments. Otherwise, helpful people have published Viking and pre-Viking cutting diagrams on various blogs and on Pinterest. Also, the Society for Creative Anachronism's Viking re-enactment society is a mine of useful information.

Shopping list

Probably the best way forward, if realism is what you are after, is to make a list of available ingredients that would have been around, and to work from there. So, at the risk of stating the obvious – no artificial fibres, no synthetic dyes, no zips or buttons. The very earliest garments were basically T-shapes, which moulded to the body with wear. Dyes were very primitive, so the colouring of the garments should be earth and vegetable shades. Available materials were wool and linen; nettles were turned into fibre too, I believe. In fact, a soft but roughish cotton and even silk noil or bourette silk is entirely convincing as a substitute for old linen, but if accuracy is important to you, you might want to leave such heresies to slightly later time frames. See page 220 for a list of suppliers.

Right Patched tunic from the Kragelund Bog.

Opposite Original 1920s dropped-waist dresses.

MEDIEVAL PERIOD (C.1100–1453)

The clothes of the centuries between the Viking period and the Renaissance developed from the simplest garments in plain wools, to the complex fashions of the age of chivalry, to the rise of the royal courts of Europe and court dress. A by-product of the religious military campaigns known as the Crusades, in the eleventh to thirteenth centuries, which took knights on forays to Jerusalem and the Near East, was the great leap in sophistication of both textiles and decoration, thanks to the silken influence of Islam.

SOME PREVIOUS CORONATIONS—KING HENRY IV

Fashion

Above The coronation of King Henry IV, with the figures dressed in rich jewel colours.

Back in Europe, the concept of romantic love as expressed by the courtly knights encouraged aristocratic women to change from dumpy quails to dazzling birds of paradise perched on dainty pedestals. While lower-class men and women wore simple wools and, if they were lucky, coarse linen, the upper classes had access to the finest linens, velvets and brocades, exquisite embroidery and, of course, the finest imported Eastern silk. At this time, the best silk was literally worth its weight in gold.

Gothic Costume, 12th to 14th Centuries

Left Max Tilke's illustrations of gothic costume.

Costume historian James Laver suggests that the mid-fourteenth century marks the emergence of recognizable 'fashion' in clothing. Before this time all garments were functional, simply to keep people warm and decently covered. The draped cloaks and straight lines of previous centuries were replaced by curved seams and the beginnings of tailoring, which allowed clothing to fit the human form more closely. The use of lacing and buttons also assisted with a snug fit. A slender figure began to be much admired, so fasting was practised by fashionable women (I wonder what those misogynist monks, who fasted only for God, thought of that), and tightly laced fine leather corsets were introduced to ensure a sinuous silhouette.

ARMOUR.

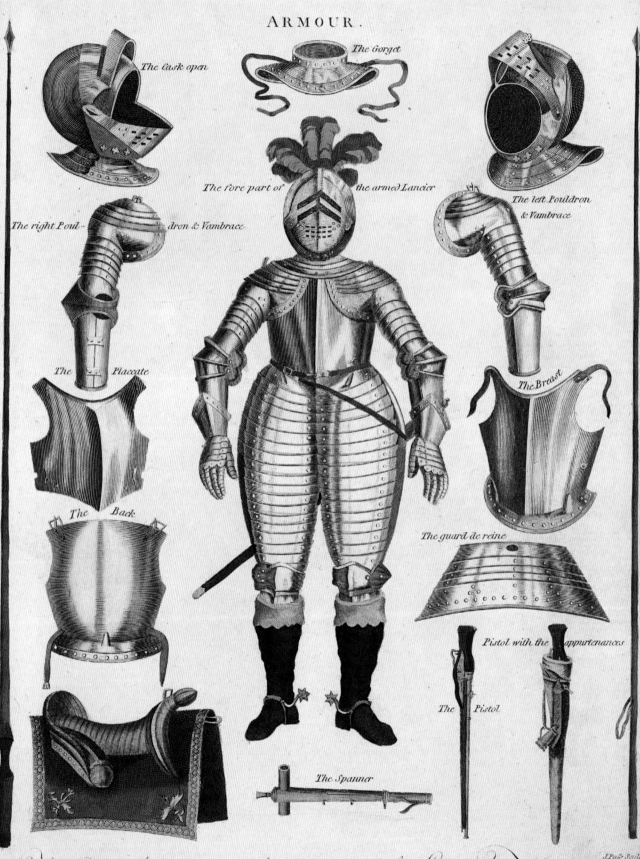

The Cask open

The Gorget

The fore part of   the armed Lancier

The left Pouldron & Vambrace

The right Poul-   dron & Vambrace

The   Placcate

The Breast

The   Back

The guard de reine

Pistol with the appurtenances

The   Pistol

The Spanner

J. Pass Sculp.

The Plate Armour and Accoutrements of a Lancier or Knight.

London Published as the Act directs Aug 31. 1793 by J. Wilkes.

Armour

And then there is the dreaded problem of knights in shining (or rusty) armour. Armour is extremely expensive, as the real thing always was. There is the example of a basic suit of armour commissioned in 1546 by a German king for his son. For this, the court armourer, Jörg Seusenhofer of Innsbruck, received the enormous sum of more than 1,200 gold coins on completion a year later, equivalent to twelve times the annual salary of a senior court official.

Nowadays, if you are into re-enactment, it is possible to buy convincing replica armour for between £800 (plain) and £3,900 (kingly), as well as all sorts of weaponry, such as stage and re-enactment swords with blunt blades (conforming to health and safety standards). Therefore, for reasons of cost alone, unless you are making a film about medieval warfare or taking part in a re-enacted tournament festival, for most stage and screen purposes the real clanking metal is probably best given a very wide berth.

Armies

When a designer has an army to deal with, there are a number of options. Many older plays, especially those of Shakespeare, involve a battle of some kind and these need to be demonstrated as convincingly as possible. On film, the teeming hordes can be multiplied on the computer (CGI), but on stage this isn't an option. So if full armour is impossible, what should you do?

One very effective way forward for the officers and lords is to use a uniform of a basic doublet and breeches or trousers tucked into boots, worn with a simple breastplate and finished with a sweeping greatcoat. I have used this solution for plays set in many centuries; no one seems to notice that the greatcoat is an anachronism because it looks so impressive. The breastplates can be made of vacuum-formed plastic covered with metallized leather, or cast in fibreglass that has been mixed with metal powders.

Above Drawing of a breastplate and greatcoat costume for *Henry IV*.

Opposite The suit of armour as worn by a medieval knight.

Left Beautifully reconstructed armour for the television series *Game of Thrones*.

The issue of the soldier is a very good reason for updating a design concept, because although large hire companies stock uniforms of almost all periods by the dozen, which it makes perfect sense to use on a film, for a long run on the stage this may not be an option. The solution I came up with for the common soldiers on Richard III at The Old Globe in San Diego

was to put them in purchased combat jackets and pants, bought quite cheaply from a military catalogue, and to give them breastplates and helmets from security personnel catalogues. We gave these a coating of smoky metallic spray and away they went. It must be said I was grateful for the smoke machines and the explosive lighting flashes, because some of the outfits didn't really bear close scrutiny when the actors were standing still in full light. However, the actors did very well considering there were only sixteen of them to demonstrate two armies and half of them were quite short girls!

The plays

This is the time frame when a number of our greatest dramas were set, many involving historical but semi-mythical personages. Shakespeare's plays *Macbeth* and *King Lear* are based on historical personages largely referenced in the pages of the chronicler Holinshed. The real King Macbeth of Scotland died in 1057 and the English King Leir, inspiration for Lear, lived about a century later. The story used by Richard Wagner of the doomed lovers *Tristan and Isolde* is set in the early thirteenth century. The plays about kings from olden times by Shakespeare and Christopher Marlowe are also set in a historic past, so it is worth considering how these dramas might be approached.

Left A production of *Henry VIII* at the Royal Shakespeare Theatre.

Below A sketch of Lear on the blasted heath.

Putting on the real thing is expensive, highly labour-intensive and hard to do well. Shakespeare's Globe Theatre in London does it, because giving the audience an experience as close as possible to theatre as it was in the sixteenth century is this theatre's whole purpose, but for everyone else a less academic approach may be the only way forward.

Period patterns

It is beyond the scope of this book to give complex period patterns, so there is a list of many terrific books with all that information in the Appendix (see page 219). However, I should mention the costume-maker's bible here, in the shape of Janet Arnold's series of books: you cannot go far wrong with these. Apart from photographs and scale patterns, she draws garments from the inside, so you can see exactly how everything, from ruffs to pluderhosen, was actually constructed. Her descriptions of grave clothes, in all their rotting detail, are a particular delight!

However, here are diagrams for a simple suit of doublet and breeches and a plain dress, which will give you a useful place to start. As they used to say in the bossier 1950s fashion magazines about little black cocktail frocks, 'These can be dressed up or down'.

Delaroche pinxit.   Hargrave sculpsit.

OLIVIER CROMWELL.

Born 1599.   Died 3th 7^{ber} 1658.

The Commonwealth period: Great Britain

Most of this book is concerned with the designing of costumes for dramas conceived at a particular time in history, and since for at least the first 60 years of the seventeenth century it appears that very little was happening in the theatre or opera, it was not until the first draft was complete that this large gap became apparent. This situation was for very good reasons. In Britain there was an all consuming Civil War (1642–51), a series of armed conflicts and political problems between Parliamentarians (Roundheads) and Royalists (Cavaliers).

The English Civil War led to the trial and execution of Charles I, the exile of his son, Charles II, and replacement of English monarchy with Britain's first republic, known as the Commonwealth of England (1649–59), under Oliver Cromwell's personal rule. Cromwell and his officers were extreme Protestants, Puritans with both a small and a capital P, and one of his first political acts was to close and sometimes raze all the country's theatres as 'dens of Satan'. All forms of theatrical and musical entertainment were forbidden, no court masques, no theatre performances, no opera or ballet to take the people's minds off their religious duties.

Opposite Oliver Cromwell in a majestic plumed hat.

Right English Royalist soldiers wearing doublet and breeches and bucket-top boots.

The Colonial period: North America

In the New World, there was definitely no time for frivolity either, but for the powerful reason that people were totally preoccupied with the business of survival.

The first European ships landed in Chesapeake Bay in 1607. The Colonial period is considered to run from the founding of Jamestown, Virginia in the same year until the war of Independence (1775 –83). To begin, these first immigrants were men, many of them adventurers lured to the New World by stories of riches and easy financial reward. The last thing they expected was to have to do hard physical work.

They were brought up to be 'gentlemen'. This meant that most of them had no useful survival skills at all except that of killing things and ordering other chaps about. And little idea of how to work for a living. All the useful domestic crafts such as cooking, sewing, mending and washing would have been carried out by women or servants, and more outdoor crafts, such as farming, carpentry, glass-making and house building by artisans and working people. The early years were tough indeed; half the arrivals in Jamestown died in that first severe winter. Other boats arrived with people and equipment that enabled the little colony to establish itself despite the mosquitoes, the relationships with the Native Indian population, the 'starving time' of 1610 and several fires that destroyed the hastily constructed wooden buildings along with most of their clothes.

It became apparent that these men, tough though they were, needed a support system to survive, and slowly women were brought out, as were artisans and craftspeople. The *Mayflower* with its cargo of brave Protestant fundamentalists landed in New England in 1620 and in the 1630s and '40s at least 20,000 people immigrated to the New England area. They were mostly yeoman families, and these sturdy, hardworking people made a great success of their new life. They were farmers, hunters and artisans and craftspeople of all kinds. While the New Englanders were governed by Puritan Boston, the Dutch settlers of New Amsterdam – New York as it became – had a more laid-back attitude to life. They enjoyed much more dancing and music-making, a way of life that was reflected in more colourful clothes.

Costume for the Commonwealth and the Colonial period

The point of this historical digression is to explain why the costume design emphasis in this period is totally removed from the theatre and is entirely concerned with 'real life'. Many films, historical dramas and documentaries deal with this crucial phase in our history, so it's as well to understand what was going on as a basis for how people dressed.

At the start of the seventeenth century a man's suit of clothes consisted of doublet, breeches and cape or casaque. This was worn over a linen long-tailed shirt, linen under-pants, stockings, shoes or boots, a hat and, if wealthy, gloves. The doublet was the main upper-body garment that men had worn from the medieval era until the 1630s when it evolved into a coat. Doublets were much the same shape as a modern jeans jacket, but longer in the waist and with more padding.

As in the British Shakespearean period breeches at the beginning of the seventeenth century were very short and wide, and padded with straw and horse-hair, finished with a tight thigh bands called 'canions'. They were known as 'trunk hose'. By 1615, breeches were much longer and less padded, but still cut very full, almost to the knee, where they were finished with a narrow band. Until 1620 or so the breeches were laced to the waistband of the doublet using tags that you could see from the outside; afterwards hooks sewn to the inside of the waistband were used. The breeches were usually interlined with a wool material and lined with linen cut straight to hold the baggy outer shape in place. They must have been cosy and warm in winter but unpleasantly hot and scratchy in the mosquito-ridden Virginian summer, and so evolved quite quickly into something more relaxed, no doubt by shedding their under-pinnings.

Women's dress in the 17th century

Girls' and women's dress in the first part of the seventeenth century consisted of a linen chemise, or under-smock, always white or natural colour, to survive vigorous washing; this garment had a round neck with a drawstring and square cut sleeves. It was knee length or a bit longer and seldom removed as very few women wore, or even possessed separate night-gowns. Under-pants or drawers were not worn, being considered indecent.

Over this came a corset, rigidly boned, with split whale bone, flat steel strips or bunches of thin dried reeds all encased in stitched channels. A padded hip roll cheerfully called a bum-roll, held out the skirts over which came one or two petticoats or underskirts, and a long full

Left Dame Judi Dench plays Elizabeth I in *Shakespeare in Love*.
The film's costumes were designed by Sandy Powell.

gathered or cartridge pleated skirt. The tight-sleeved bodice fastened in front, with metal hooks and bars, or with laces in the two seams that shaped the back of the garment.

Women would have a warm cloak, knitted or bias cut wool hose held up with garters, and sturdy leather shoes with low stacked heels. Hair was simply wound up in a bun and covered at all times by a linen cap, and topped, when out of doors, or in church, by a black felt hat.

The importance of black

The ordinary people wore less black than our image of the Pilgrim Fathers and Mothers would have us believe. In many portraits of that time, people are shown wearing black because firstly, only important people had their pictures painted, and secondly, the sitters liked to wear their best clothes which, in the 1620s, were often black.

However, black certainly was favoured by important people in the community. Church ministers, governors and judges would wear it most of the time. Not only did it emphasize seriousness and authority, but it was as far removed as possible from the gaudy colours of the

Below The cast of 1996 film adaptation of *The Crucible* clad in black.

royal courts and the jewel-bright clothes of the Royalist Cavaliers.

This tendency to black is a great gift to the costume designer; it always looks good. In fact everyday clothes were made of many colours. All shades of brown, from brick and russet to darkest mulberry, red made from madder roots, yellows, soft blues from woad and indigo, and gentle greens were popular. Other clothes were made of cloth that was not dyed. These clothes were grey, brown, or white, the natural colour of the cloth, from unbleached linen, which is a nice brown-paper envelope colour or brown wool from the charming multi-coloured breed known as 'Jacob's sheep'.

It was not easy to dye cloth the solid, long-lasting black that was so much in demand for formal garments. It was a difficult dye to work, one recipe involves iron oxide sometimes derived from rusty nails or steel wool and vinegar, often used for leather; another version uses oak gall. Black also tended to fade to a strange mildewed green with age and exposure to sunlight, or a rusty brown, depending on the recipe.

Men's clothes

The doublet and short breeches had been abandoned by 1620 and men wore a suit of garments made from wool or leather, with a wool cloak. Hair was quite long and many men wore a moustache and trimmed pointed beard in a style known as a 'Van Dyke'.

The doublet morphed into the coat. Much of the padding and interfacing was discarded to make a softer line. The little tabs of the basque became just four pieces – two at the front and two at the back – and grew to mid-thigh, a useful jacket length. Jacket sleeves which had developed from the casaque were still open along the front seam. They were adorned with many buttons to expose the full-sleeved shirt.

The ruff collapsed, lost its fullness and then became a simple linen or lace collar tied with a small tasselled cord. Breeches were full and baggy, fastening just below the knee.

It will be clear from the preceding section that, unlike the stage-based inspiration of much else in this book, these are the garments of ordinary people, the simplest versions of classic period shapes, and as such can be applied to many different costume schemes. This is where the re-enactment societies with their splendid catalogues and craft fairs really come into their own on both sides of the Atlantic.

RESTORATION TO REGENCY (1660–1820)

There are two main reasons why a production would be set in any particular time frame. Firstly because said period is the date of composition, and secondly because the creative team have decided to set a play or opera in a different, nearly always later, period. As I have stated elsewhere, the clothes of the seventeenth and eighteenth century are complex, expensive and hard to get right. But it is very satisfying to have a go! Restoration drama, such as the witty, sexy plays of Congreve, Wycherley and Sheridan, is quite dependent on an understanding of social placement and the audience really gain from a full understanding of the period. In my opinion, many nuances of response can be lost using, let us say, casual, twenty-first century clothes.

Wigs

Below **Below** Towering wigs worn by the cast of *The Cladestine Marriage*.

My earlier remarks about complexity and expense are also applicable to this time frame, with the added difficulty of the gentlemen's periwig – a bizarre fashion that held men in its hairy grip for 200 years. It must have been hard enough to keep infestations of tiny creatures out of your own locks without capping your head with wodges of not very clean hair culled from horses'

tails and plague victims (when the supply of willing nuns ran out). On top of that, the eighteenth-century addition of white powder – aka flour – must have intensified the opportunities for cranial irritation.

Unless you are making a specific point, have a very large budget, or are doing Peter Shaffer's play *Amadeus* or a film about Charles II, I would suggest exploring simpler alternatives.

Wig tricks

I once saw an opera chorus wearing simple eighteenth-century dresses and small wig caps, which looked very neat and appropriate. I'm fond of headscarf turbans tied at the back of the head myself, a solution that works well for many periods, and sock hats are also useful. The actor's own hair, nicely dressed, looks good too, maybe with the addition of a 'piece' or back fall to finish off the look. If you really need big wigs, those made of nylon hair, properly dressed, are a surprisingly good solution. Don't buy the white ones: they will look like cotton wool under the lights; streaky light grey is much better. Men's seventeenth-century long wigs never have enough hair in them and are much too small, so buy two per person and stitch them together. Artificial hair is usually far too shiny to be convincing, but you can spray it with lacquer and powder it down a bit.

Basic eighteenth-century outfits

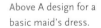

Above A design for a basic maid's dress.

Women

The woman's dress is dependent upon a well-fitted corset bodice; you can, of course, make a proper corset and put the dress on top, but to actually bone the bodice as if it were a corset works very well instead. It also does away with any fuss on the part of the performer, who might be disposed to grumble about tight lacing.

The trick for making these dresses is to put enough material in the skirt and add a simple hip roll and/or substantial underskirts to give the dress a proper swagger. This is where ready-made dresses from a catalogue or re-enactment site usually prove unsatisfactory: the boned top is likely to be not nearly tight enough, and the skirts way too meagre.

You can add pretty lace cuffs and an embroidered underskirt for upper-class characters or leave the dress plain, with the skirt hitched up to reveal a striped cotton petticoat, for everyone else. This combo seems to work every time.

Men

Men's costume at this period can be just as ornamented as that of the ladies, and for short stage
runs and screen work it is probably sensible to rent. However, it is possible to buy excellent
outfits from re-enactment catalogues such as that of Jas. Townsend in the US (a fascinating read,
by the way). It's not so easy in the UK, but the Historical Re-enactor's Society holds twice-yearly
markets near Coventry, where many makers of both costume and artefacts can be found.

A basic suit of men's clothes is not too challenging and, made up from a good pattern in a
well-chosen fabric, will look very good. I would suggest using a severely limited range of both
fabric and colour. I don't know why this uniform approach should be so effective in making
a costume scheme look smart and so much more expensive than it actually was, but on the
occasions that I have incorporated this method I have been delighted with the results. Good
fabrics to use are undyed cottons from suppliers such as Whaleys of Bradford, or Fucotex in
Germany, who will supply a hefty cotton sateen for men's coats, and mattress ticking, cotton
denim or medium-weight curtain lining and calico for everything else.

The Regency period (1811–20)

In Britain the Regency period lasted from 1811–20 and was contemporary with the Empire style in France. These neoclassical styles saw a revival of interest in all things Greek and Egyptian.

Women

Women's costume suddenly became very simple, a style that lasted for about 30 years. Clinging Indian muslins took the place of stiff silk taffetas; pretty, pashmina-type shawls were worn instead of tailored jackets; and soft, ballet-style flats replaced chunky boots. The young and fairly flat-chested can get away without wearing corsets – just. You can even buy ready-made paper patterns for this period from companies such as Simplicity and Butterick.

Men

Men, on the other hand, are far more difficult to dress, because as clothes became plainer, the geometric art of the gentleman's tailor took precedence over the rather softer approach that had survived for so long. Smart men began to wear long trousers instead of breeches. These were either high-waisted and skintight (which looked terrific when on a horse or as part of an army uniform), or carrot-shaped, 'peg-topped' pants, which were considered more dandified. Gentlemen began to wear the severely tailored frock coat in ever darker colours, a fashion that morphed into the two- or three-piece suits still with us for formal wear today.

Right Designs for basic sprigged dresses.

In the early 1800s, the Napoleonic Wars engulfed or threatened much of Europe, and as a result military uniforms were everywhere. These uniforms were highly ornate and for the officers at least, covered in yards of bullion (metallic gold or silver) braid, frogging, aiguillettes (not to be confused with lanyards), epaulettes and weaponry. Towering kepis or helmets topped with cockerel feathers and/or plumes made of dyed hair from horses' tails completed the outfit. As might be imagined, knowledge of military uniforms needs highly specialized study: retired colonels become outraged and write to complain if you get it wrong!

Early nineteenth-century works

In the early 1800s, there was a fashion for historical dramas and operas involving extravagant spectacle, often complete with on-stage horses and rabbits, not to mention real rainstorms. They were usually set in a semi-mythical past, and from what we can see, it seems unlikely that there was much call for contemporary costume.

But if there was a shortage of stage works written about the early nineteenth century, this is more than made up for by the many novels of the period, which have formed the genesis of multiple film and television productions. The works of Jane Austen, Elizabeth Gaskell, William Thackeray and Charles Dickens seem to provide a never-ending supply of material. Also, the Regency (and the Victorian) period in general is enthusiastically explored for naturalistic docu-dramas. In these cases, it is hard to imagine any creative team being rash enough to mess with the period settings, because the social history aspect is the source of the drama. But with operas by composers such as Wagner and Bellini or even early Verdi – who are not dealing with domestic subjects where folk take afternoon tea and worry about their bonnets – designers have much more freedom to reinterpret the drama for their own times.

Left Braided uniforms worn in the film adaptation of *Vanity Fair*.

Costuming a production

The need to produce historically convincing sets of costumes is a challenge. For once, I don't think there is much of an alternative to making the leading ladies' dresses and hiring more or less everything else. However, it is well worthwhile spending time and creativity on the accessories. For the men, really nice waistcoats are hard to find in rental shops and they are straightforward enough to make in attractively coloured embroidered silk. Finding smart neckwear to rent can also be an issue. It is tricky to maintain, for a start, requiring sophisticated laundering techniques that have almost been forgotten in this easy-care polyester age, and rummaging through sagging boxes in even the best rental shops or theatre stockrooms is usually a depressing experience. If you spend time sourcing/making starched white collars and generous, clean cravats, it will make the outfits. A black or dark navy frock coat will not reveal if it is past its sell-by date, but a shabby, creased or too-low collar, and a skimpy, fake cravat most certainly will. Women's hats are another item that deteriorates rapidly in storage. Imagine trying to keep large flower arrangements in good shape in cramped conditions without them getting squashed or bent out of shape – it's the same with decorated hats and bonnets.

In times when clothing was, compared to today, extremely costly, all but the very wealthy would make use of a plain dress, nicely made, but with ever-changing accessories. This was actually how people went about organizing their wardrobes at the time. I followed this principle for the film *Mrs Brown* (see next section).

Below Smartening the neckwear before a performance of *Napoli*.

THE VICTORIAN PERIOD (1837–1901)

I'm afraid there is no getting away from the fact that to make realistic upper-class costumes from the nineteenth and early twentieth centuries, you need an abundant supply of time, skill and money.

Above An array of regal Victorian costume in *The Young Victoria*.

Cut your costs

There are ways to reduce costs, however. You could do clever schemes such as dressing everyone in a single colour in inexpensive fabric topped with an outrageous hat, rather as Cecil Beaton did to memorable effect in the Ascot scene of the 1964 film of *My Fair Lady* (not that any of the fabrics Beaton used were inexpensive, but you get the point).

You can deliberately change the period, as is done in many opera productions. In the 2012 production of Hector Berlioz's *Les Troyens* (The Trojans) at Covent Garden, both armies were clad in greatcoats over simple vests and dark trousers tucked into boots. I have an unworthy suspicion that all the money went on the spectacular scrap metal Trojan horse's head that dominates the stage and the costumes were a bit of an afterthought, but the production was still hugely impressive.

The 1997 film *Mrs Brown*, about Queen Victoria, was made on a very low budget. As the queen, Judi Dench had two dresses, one in cotton for when she was miserable, and a more ornate one in silk for when she was feeling rather better. I found and made an assortment of collars, caps, bonnets and veils to ring the changes, and no one ever noticed that she hadn't had a new frock for twenty years. It helped that Queen Victoria only wore black, of course.

Mid- to late nineteenth century

The plays of many playwrights working during the second part of the nineteenth century are regularly performed today, the best known being Oscar Wilde, George Bernard Shaw and Anton Chekhov. Much of what I wrote about the Regency period applies here, with the added difficulty that the women's dresses are even more complex; also the writers, Wilde in particular, are wont to show aristocratic people attending posh parties. To do this attractively is seldom a cheap option. Assuming you have the budget to make some costumes, there is a great richness of available reference material to be found.

Paintings and photographs

Portrait painters such as Queen Victoria's favourite painter, Franz Winterhalter, and later on, James Jacques Joseph Tissot, John Singer Sargent and Giovanni Boldini can provide great inspiration. Winterhalter and Tissot, in particular, are terrific costume painters. If you can make your scheme look like the work of either of these painters, you will have achieved great things (you will need the help of the lighting designer here). Tissot was painting in the 1870s, when high fashion for ladies consisted of row upon row of frills over swaying bustles and the tightest of corsets – hard to do well (but this shape could make fabulous ballet costumes when made in feather-light fabrics such as muslin or organza). It's quite a relief that men's evening dress was black and more black, only enlivened with white.

Opposite Dame Judi Dench on the set of *Mrs Brown*.

PORTRAIT GALLERY OF BRITISH COSTUME

July 1870

Published with the "TAILOR AND CUTTER" by JOHN WILLIAMSON, 93, Drury Lane London W.

From 1850 onwards came the new invention of photography. It is a revelation to see how people actually looked compared to the somewhat idealized images of the painted portrait. The state and condition of people's hair in those days before detergent shampoo is quite greasily revealing. The *carte de visite* of Gaspard-Felix Tournachon, known as Nadar, is extremely interesting. Have a look at Nadar's 1865 revolving self-portrait: it's amazing (http://en.wikipedia.org/wiki/File:Nadar_autoportrait_tournant.gif)! Photographs are invaluable if your project needs to display convincing social realism.

I would love to see a truly realistic production of Puccini's *La Bohème*, with those freezing students, street scenes and poor little grisette, Mimi. But there is something about opera singers that is always too sumptuous, too colourful, to actually suggest the squalid living conditions of low-rent nineteenth-century Paris.

Books

However useful old photographs are, you may need more technical information than is visible in a faded black and white image, and this is where the pattern books of the often mentioned Janet Arnold and anything by Nora Waugh are indispensible. These publications are crucial if you are confused by the often wildly idealized paintings of Sargent and company. Dover Publications produces a substantial range of vintage catalogues from establishments such as Bloomingdale's and Sears, Roebuck and Company, and trade-cum-social journals such as the invaluable *Tailor & Cutter*. The engraved drawings tend to look a bit wooden, but you can really see what is going on.

Above left An immensely useful reference book of original engravings showing nineteenth-century mens' clothing.

THE TWENTIETH CENTURY

Above Paul Poiret's clothes
drawn by Georges Lepape, 1911.

In the first decade of the century, the breaking open of the puritan repressiveness that was the
hallmark of the Victorian era was set vigorously in motion. The designer who epitomized this new
freedom in fashion was the French couturier Paul Poiret. He released women from the bondage of
the steel-boned corset, made cropped hair fashionable and even invented the bra. He is on record
as remarking that if he had realized that the billowing curves of the fashionable woman would be
lost forever, he would have taken more notice of them while they lasted! An incidental side effect of
the new styles was that ten-course meals went out of fashion, because the figures that resulted from
them could only be controlled by industrial-strength lacing.

The Edwardians

The Edwardian period before the First World War of 1914–18 is regarded as a lost golden age. Popular TV series such as *Downton Abbey* (2010 onwards) and *Upstairs Downstairs* (1971–75 and 2010–12) amply demonstrate that if you were well off and lived somewhere attractive, life was very good, but working people and the poor had to scrape by as usual.

The fashions of the first years of the twentieth century are possibly my all-time favourites. My first job at the Royal Court Theatre, London, in the late 1960s, was to design the costumes for three plays about D.H. Lawrence's home town mining community, set in 1912. Even the working-class costumes had a sort of elegance and dignity about them.

If you are fortunate enough to be asked to design costumes for this period, whether the project is of this time or because you have decided to set a play in the Edwardian era, there is plenty of reference material available. Photographs, portrait paintings and even fashion plates can easily be found. The director Ian Judge, designer John Gunter and I set a production of Shakespeare's *Love's Labour's Lost* in an Oxford college just before the outbreak of the First World War, partly because we just liked it, but also because the story fitted perfectly with the sense of impending loss that hangs over it all. We even ended the evening with the boys looking out to the lowering horizon while the noise of the guns drew ever closer.

The First World War and its aftermath (1914–20)

No one could have predicted the horrifying consequences of using modern weaponry together with out-of-date tactics in a war run by incompetent generals, and the casualty numbers send shivers down the spine. It is thought that the Allies, including Great Britain and America, lost around 5 million men, and the Central Powers, which included Germany and Austria, 3.3 million. How ironic that the 'winners' lost more men than the losers. The war was followed by a pandemic of Spanish flu, which killed tens of thousands more.

Opposite The ladies of *Love's Labour's Lost* in Edwardian-style costume at the RSC.

Uniforms

Wars mean uniforms, multitudes of them: military of all ranks and nations, ambulance crews, Women's Land Army, Queen Alexandra's Imperial Military Nursing Service, civilian uniforms such as police and fire services, and those of men and women driving trains and collecting tickets on buses. Any production involving the history of this time, any plays and operas that have been updated to this 1914–18 wartime time frame (and it happens quite often), will need a ready supply of accurate uniforms.

Angels the Costumiers (Morris Angel & Son) in London probably has the largest selection of European uniforms in the UK, if not globally. Western Costume in Los Angeles is also well equipped, as is The History Bunker in Leeds, UK. Don't even think of making the things: they come hung about with so many details such as puttees, helmets, Sam Browne belts and goodness knows what else, that you really can't do it without specialist help. An exception might be perhaps for officers' uniforms that are supposed to be newly tailored to fit; even then I would get a proper military tailor to make them, and you will still need the boots and the belts.

Civilian clothing

'Fashion', as we understand the term, doesn't get a look-in during major wars. Rationing wasn't actually introduced until towards the end of the war, but 'consumables' were in short supply, and it was considered unpatriotic to flaunt wealth by wearing frivolous clothes when 'our boys' were undergoing such terrible hardships. When you think that in the UK, 35 per cent of the men who went to fight were killed or injured, everyone would have had a family member (or known of someone) who was killed, injured or missing.

Below Land girls photographed during WWI wearing their work uniform of smocks and sturdy boots.

The 1920s

It is hardly surprising that fashion in the 1920s was characterized by a brittle glamour, not seen before or to be seen again until the miniskirts of the 'swinging sixties'. After the war, the fashionable ideal ceased to be the grown-up woman with curves, and the girl who looked more like an adolescent boy was introduced.

Above The flapper dress is synonymous with the look of the 1920s.

If there was a craze of this era it was dance – the Charleston was perhaps the best-known example. Maybe uninhibited dancing helped to blank out the more depressing aspects of life, as exemplified by Fred and Adele Astaire's song and dance number 'I'd Rather Charleston'. Many other dances were based on politer versions of exotic Afro-Caribbean or Latino originals.

Work and leisure

Life was exceptionally tough for the poor of both Europe and America, and when life is hard you don't have the money or energy for anything as unnecessary as fashion. Work clothes for both sexes remained much the same throughout the period, except that women and girls cut their hair and their skirts to copy popular actresses from the movie magazines.

Right Edward VIII in golfing attire, photographed with Crown Prince Hirohito in Japan.

For men, their pin-up came in the tiny form of the Prince of Wales who was, it seems, almost single-handedly responsible for introducing the concept of smart 'leisurewear'. His appearance on a Scottish golf course one day in a hand-knitted Fair Isle jumper, tweed jacket and plus fours not only started a trend in hand and machine knitting that lasted until the 1980s, but revived a whole industry into the bargain.

Women

Women's dresses were very simple, with drop waists and quite free of shaping seams or darts. They are indeed very easy to make. You can find originals even now, but a 90-year-old dress is going to be far too fragile to survive anything other than a day or two's shooting. However, it is worthwhile looking at such things if only to get an idea of the proportions and to use as

patterns. The challenge with creating a convincing 1920s look is finding suitably lightweight fabrics for the dresses. Evening wear in particular used fine chiffons, often embroidered with beads or sequins, exquisitely hand stitched. It can be done, but it does cost.

Hair

By 1926, almost every woman under the age of 60 had cropped her hair, and attempted to diet away her childbearing hips and flatten any bosom that she might have possessed. Men's hair was even shorter. I emphasize the small head/hair issue because it is a real problem for the costume designer these days. You can insist that the men have the obligatory 'short back and sides', but very few actresses or singers will sacrifice their tumbling locks just to play a part. Very short wigs, where the nape of the neck is exposed, are almost impossible to achieve effectively and they seldom – no, never – move as freely as real hair. I don't really have a solution to this; if a leading lady will not have a haircut, you can only do your best with the shortest wig possible and make use of bandeaux. With extras, you can dress the hair very tightly to the head and then stick a hat or bandeau (again) over it to good effect.

Below The ghosts of *Die tote Stadt* in 1920s-inspired costumes.

The 1930s

Clothes shapes softened considerably during the 1930s. Although fashion was led by the great Parisian couturiers, particularly Coco Chanel and Madeleine Vionnet, Hollywood movies provided glamorous escapist inspiration. This proved to be much needed, with the twin disasters of the Great Depression in the USA and the gathering storm clouds in Europe that erupted into the Second World War in 1939.

Men

Upper-class men who were politicians and city types still wore the black cutaway coat, striped morning trousers and stiff collars of an earlier age, but the tailored three-piece suit became increasingly popular with other men, save for the Bohemian set, who favoured hairy tweed jackets, jumpers and corduroy trousers worn with a soft shirt, and the working classes, who wore ancient work suits and scarves as they had done since the Victorian era. Hollywood led the way in America with tremendous smartly tailored leisurewear, blazers, wide-legged flannels, and open-neck, soft-collared shirts. There was also dedicated sportswear for manly sports such as tennis, riding and swimming.

Women

Two new inventions which changed the way women looked were the permanent wave, which basically toasted the hair into a controlled series of tight ridges, and Madame Vionnet's discovery that soft fabric cut on the bias clung seductively to a woman's figure in the most elegant way. Cutting on the bias (or cross) like this exposed every unwanted lump and bulge, so despite these new dresses' free appearance, seriously engineered underpinnings were required to achieve a smooth line.

1930s productions

There have been some superb productions set in the 1930s, notably the British TV series of Agatha Christie's *Hercule Poirot* stories (1989–2013) – an absolute object lesson in how to do it well. (A number of designers are credited, including Sheena Napier, Linda Mattock and Charlotte Holdich.) Another brilliantly costumed production was Fellini's film *Tea With Mussolini* (1999), with costumes by Jenny Beavan, Anna Anni and Alberto Spiazzi.
As well as productions that are set in this period, all sorts of plays from the era are still performed, such as the works of Noël Coward, T.S. Eliot, Clifford Odets and Eugene O'Neill. These plays are usually styled as for the period of writing, but be prepared to update if needs be.

Opposite Fashion plates show typical 1930s dresses.

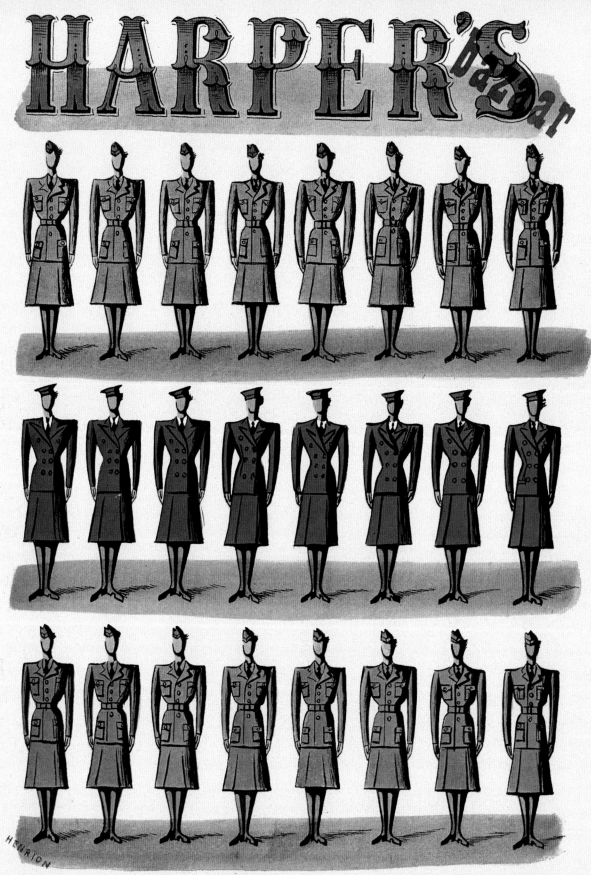

HARPER'S bazaar

The Second World War (1939–45)

In the Second World War, rationing struck almost immediately, starting with fuel in 1939, quickly followed in 1940 by many foods and then fabric and clothing. Ration books containing coupons were issued, and these had to be presented in order to buy rationed goods. Clothes didn't cease to need coupons until 1949, petrol the following year and the final ration books were not torn up until sugar, sweets and finally butter became freely available in 1953–54. Rationing had lasted for fourteen long years. America entered the war in 1942, greatly to the Allies' relief, and rationing started in the US almost immediately.

I mention rationing because the shortages governed how everyone looked all over Europe and, to slightly less all-pervading effect, in the United States. For those not in a uniform of some kind, 'make do and mend' was the watchword.

Uniforms

The war effort was greatly aided by an organization formed in 1938 by Stella Isaacs, Lady Reading, known as the WVS (Women's Voluntary Service). These ladies had a non-compulsory, but very smart, dark green uniform designed by the Queen's couturier, Norman Hartnell. They were undaunted by any emergency – Lady Reading had a simple philosophy for the WVS: if the job needed doing, it was done.

1940s costumes

When assembling 1940s costumes, it's worth working hard to get the sense of rationing and restriction right. Although very few people will notice if a woman has got a 10cm (4in) hem instead of the regulation 5cm (2in), or has too many pleats in her skirt, if you get it right you will create a believable picture of reality that will be very moving. Images of an entire community struggling together will add greatly to any production.

Opposite *Harper's Bazaar* cover from 1942 makes uniform look almost glamorous.

Below Actress Keira Knightley wears bias cut silk on the set of *Atonement*, set in the period running up to, and during, WWII.

Of course, older people simply wore clothes that they already possessed, altered as necessary. Men's suits were made to last for generations (and wives could even get a pattern that showed you how to make a lady's suit out of one your husband's). And those 1930s wool crêpe dresses were pretty indestructible too.

You wouldn't set an extravagant dinner party in this period: as well as being considered unpatriotic, food rationing would have made such an event simply impossible on an allowance of 50g (2oz) of butter and one egg each per week. The British TV series *Foyle's War* (2002 onwards) is an excellent example of how to do this period really well.

Wartime entertainment

As one might imagine, entertainment was somewhat restricted. America had Hollywood's patriotic movies and cheerful vaudeville. Romantic films were a welcome escape from the harshness of the times; these were often doctored to show the war in an optimistic and noble

Right *Absolute Hell,* a play by Rodney Ackland, set in a nighclub during WWII.

light. Germany had the blackest of satirical cabarets; the UK imported American films with enthusiasm, but also produced cheering propaganda movies such as the popular and inspiring *Mrs. Miniver* (1942), starring Greer Garson and Walter Pidgeon, and *In Which We Serve* (1942), directed by and starring Noël Coward as a highly unlikely naval commander.

Allied troops were entertained by Glenn Miller's big band, and visits from singing stars, such as Vera Lynn, 'the forces' sweetheart', and Coward himself singing rousing, if sentimental, songs. At home in shabby, war-torn Britain, nightly revues with showgirls and racy nude tableaux vivants packed them in at the Windmill Theatre (post-war motto: 'We never closed'), while the indefatigable Osiris Players toured the country.

At the outbreak of war, the Osiris Players' director, Nancy Hewins, and her group of seven female actresses toured the length and breadth of Britain performing Shakespeare's plays and other British works to thousands of schoolchildren and adults, keeping spirits up and instilling a lifelong love of the theatre in many who saw them. The Players toured in a 1923 Rolls Royce and later by horse and covered wagon, sleeping where they could (digs were too expensive). In order to make ends meet, they worked as shop assistants or waitresses as well as doing over 1,500 performances of 55 plays, charging five old pennies a seat to watch seven days a week! Actress Imogen Stubbs's play *We Happy Few* (2003–4) gives a vivid account of the troupe's adventures. It would make a terrific film.

Below Actress June Brown wears an original 1940s dress on stage.

The end of the war and the 1950s

The war ended in 1945, a couple of months after the suicide of Adolf Hitler. In 1947 the Parisian couturier Christian Dior unveiled his New Look to an astonished world. These fashions, involving many yards of fabric gathered into long, swirling skirts, were met with considerable disapproval on both sides of the Atlantic.

Such extravagance was the envy of British women, still rationed to 2.25m (2½yd) of sensible tweed to make their now rather boring suits. American ladies formed 'The Little-Below-the-Knee Club' as a cross reaction to all this frippery, which they considered to be unpatriotic and not emancipated. It didn't work. The new shapes were too feminine, too exciting and just far too pretty to be resisted for long. The New Look, in its many variations, became the iconic look of the 1950s.

A new era
Naturally enough, there was an explosion of offerings in every medium: plays, films from Hollywood, Europe and the UK, and Broadway musicals. Women were encouraged to reproduce, to make up for all those lost men, which it seems they did with enthusiasm, as a baby boom resulted. Advertising promoted a slightly nauseating image of wholesome wifely perfection, where wives vacuumed the floor before smartening up in discreet make-up and

Left A 1950s New Look gown.

high heels to greet hubby when he arrived home from the office, ready with his home-cooked supper on the table, before retiring to the bedroom in a sweetly sexy nightie to engage in some more reproduction. I guess it worked for some.

1950s productions

Social history aside, the 1950s are a great source of inspiration if you are looking for an era in which to set a play or opera. You can argue that at the couture end of the market, not only was it the last truly glamorous period, but it was certainly the last time that old-fashioned feminine exploitation and repression made visual sense. (OK, so that last remark is far from the complete story, but it does have logic at its core.)

There was a very popular production in 1982 of Verdi's *Rigoletto*, which director Jonathan Miller and his costume designer, the late Rosemary Vercoe, set among the Mafia in 1950s Little Italy, Manhattan – which made perfect dramatic sense. It was infinitely more telling than both the date of composition, 1851 (crinolines and frock coats), or the time in which it was originally set, sixteenth-century Mantua (men in tights and pumpkin breeches).

I designed the costumes for a production of Offenbach's *The Tales of Hoffman* set in the 1950s (directed by Ian Judge). I was very pleased with this – the Marilyn Monroe Barbie for the robotic doll, Olympia and the showy, opera-going chorus in purples and carmines proved particularly successful. The 1950s also made an excellent point of departure for a production of *The Marriage of Figaro* directed by Adrian Noble for Opéra Lyon in 2011.

Right Design for the Duchess in *The Marriage of Figaro*.

1950s costumes

With regard to actually finding and making clothes from or inspired by the 1950s, men's clothes are probably easiest, as it is often possible to find originals in specialist vintage shops and the rental shops are full of them.

Original ladies' clothing can sometimes be found, but apart from some solidly made outerwear, it is seldom in a good enough condition to use. That said, original Jaeger suits or wool swagger coats often hold up very well. Vintage everyday dresses often look a bit dowdy, so unless downbeat social realism is what you are after, you will probably have to make them. The grand evening gowns that are such fun to use can seldom be found. If they are in really good condition, they will be very expensive and probably belong in a museum by now. However, you can make them up in a good taffeta and with the right underpinnings, they will always look splendid. Original dresses can be copied, but it is also possible to find excellent original and reproduction sewing patterns on the Internet and in good fabric shops.

Right The handsomely dressed cast of the television series, *Mad Men.*

The swinging sixties

This decade was, at least in the public memory, dominated by The Beatles, the miniskirt and the contraceptive pill. The pill, in that happy pre-AIDs era, promised unlimited freedom to have sex without unwanted consequences. Given how pop music evolved in the following decades, it seems hard to believe that The Beatles, those four rather sweet young men, could have caused such outrage with their tuneful songs, their matching collarless suits and the famous shiny, mop-headed haircuts, but they did.

The 1960s can be a rich source of inspiration for designers. It was the first period in history where the youth was more in the public eye than the older generation. I can think of many movies where the '60s-inspired designs have added immeasurably to the narrative and the audiences' enjoyment. Maybe because young people became quite rigidly divided into various 'style tribes' such as Mods, Rockers and so forth, who came with their own music as well as distinctive uniforms. The musical film *Hairspray* was a delightful, and very camp, evocation of the decade – the creative team must have had a lot of fun. The witty look of the production made it possible to tackle some interesting social issues such as race relations and body image with a light heart. Similar issues were examined on a far more serious level with the film *The Secret Life of Bees*, set in 1960s South Carolina. This was a delicate recreation of both time and place. In my opinion, it was exactly how that kind of project should be executed, with the designer taking a sensitive and self-effacing approach that lets the characters speak for themselves, unencumbered by the creative team showing off.

Miniskirts and models

The British designer Mary Quant's promotion of the miniskirt exactly caught the new spirit of youth, which totally wiped out the cult of fashion for grown-up women that had dominated couture for so long. The model Leslie Hornby, aka Twiggy, was the icon of the decade – huge eyes, cropped fair hair, and a figure like a 12-year-old boy – and was suddenly everywhere. Her tiny skirts, worn over the newly available tights, her sharp little geometric haircuts, often by Vidal Sassoon, and the fact that she wore as much eye make-up as a girl could ladle on may have horrified her elders but it was all tremendously liberating for the young. Hot pants, or very short shorts, came in towards the end of the decade, and some judges said in all seriousness that they constituted an inducement to rape.

Love and peace

Opposite Floral print shift dress with matching bag and hat, from the iconic British brand, Biba.

The 1960s had a dark side. The Vietnam War lasted from 1959 until the ignominious withdrawal of US forces in 1975. It was deeply unpopular with many, particularly the young, and the period saw the emergence of a counterculture that produced, among other movements, hippies, with their belief in a gentler, more rural existence underpinned with much cannabis, long hair, guitar music and floppy ethnic clothes.

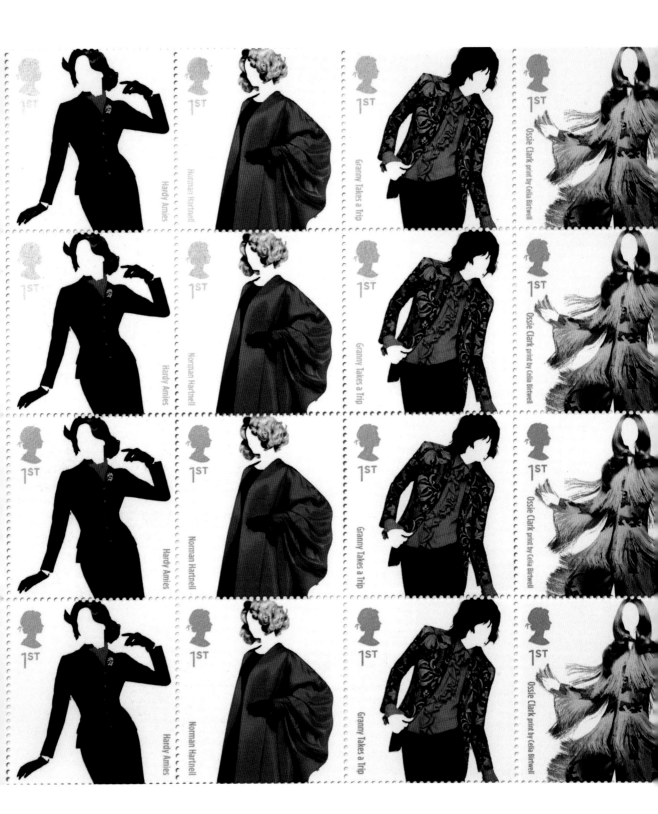

The 1970s

Many 1970s fashions were influenced by the hippie movement of the 1960s, and outfits worn by popular bands. If The Beatles epitomized the 1960s, the 'It group' of the 1970s was probably ABBA. I'm not sure that their design style was ever quite as over the top as it appeared in the

glorious finale of the film *Mamma Mia* (2008), but the slashed-to-the-waist satin shirts, the matching flares that were almost culottes, and the towering platform boots definitely summed up the era.

In some ways, the 1970s are a more fruitful source of design inspiration than the more obvious 1960s. The period worked well for me in a production at Grange Park Opera, UK of Tchaikovsky's *Eugene Onegin* in 2000.

Men

Polo-neck shirts and flower prints were characteristic 1970s looks for men. In the latter part of the decade, three-piece suits became fashionable, in large part because of the movie *Saturday*

Above The costumes worn by actress Ali MacGraw in the film
Love Story sparked many imitations and the film is still quoted as
a style inspiration today.

Left Iconic designs of the Seventies.

Night Fever (1977). Sideburns became popular, as did beards and big hair, which had been out of fashion since the nineteenth century.

Platform shoes hadn't been seen since the cork-soled creations of the 1940s, but this time around they were even higher and in much brighter colours, and worn by both sexes. (I had a rather short friend in the 1970s who, somewhat the worse for wear, fell off his 15cm/6in. platform boots and broke his ankle …)

Women

The 1970s were actually a most attractive period for many women. The return to a doe-eyed femininity appealed to many who found the 1960s' miniskirts and the gamine minidresses made from plastic discs too extreme, or were possessed of curvy hips and bosoms. We happily bought or made long, flowing lawn dresses in assorted flower prints, and enthusiastically joined a crafts revival learning useful skills such as crochet,

Above Stylish duo Mick and Bianca Jagger wed in 1971.

patchwork and macramé. The Welsh designer Laura Ashley perhaps epitomized the era much as Quant had for the 1960s.

Women's hairstyles went from long and straight in the first half of the decade to the feathery 'lion cut' of *Charlie's Angels* actress Farrah Fawcett in the TV series of 1976–81.

The 1980s and 1990s

In 1980, ex-actor Ronald Reagan became president of the United States. He and his wife Nancy spearheaded a swing to the right (which was mirrored in the UK by the election of a grocer's daughter from Grantham, Margaret Hilda Thatcher, in 1979). New Republican policies contributed to the dismantling of social welfare systems, allowing the gap between rich and poor to greatly increase. When it is fashionable to be rich, middle-aged and right wing, the more eccentric styles of the artistic or intellectual liberal are not appreciated. Shabby chic has no place in polite society! Why? Perhaps because such independence of spirit, with its refusal to conform to the boringly tidy norm, is inherently threatening to right-wing governments.

The motto of the decade was that that of fictional money man Gordon Gekko, played with chilling conviction by Michael Douglas in the 1987 movie *Wall Street*: 'Greed … is good.' It was an attitude that we are only now, in the second decade of the twenty-first century, reaping the poisoned fruits of in the shape of an all-but ruined economy on both sides of the Atlantic.

1980s chic

The shapes of the era were very distinctive: for women, there was the inverted triangle reminiscent of the American footballer. Big, rigidly styled hair topped padded shoulders that often involved three sets of pads (little ones tucked under the bra strap, slightly larger ones on a shirt or formal jacket, and outsized ones in a winter coat).

For women, the most popular skirt was straight and just above the knee, and tights were generally nude for formal, non-office wear and black at all other times. Women were increasingly entering the workplace in professions where traditionally they had not worked, and to demonstrate their seriousness wore dark, two-piece suits (a skirt suit in such professions as banking and the law, and masculine-tailored trouser suits in more relaxed professions such as advertising or film production). There was lots and lots of black, and not just for fashion assistants.

The prevailing silhouette of a decade often contrasts quite strongly with the preceding ten years, thus the narrow shoulders and long, feminine lines of the 1930s, 1950s and 1970s were all followed by sharper, more geometric garments in the 1940s, 1960s and now the 1980s. This worked for men's fashion, too: the floral shirts and velvet flares of the 1970s were abandoned for smart dark business suits and short hair in the 1980s. Older, more conservative men had always worn suits for business, however. An increasingly popular company directive of 'dress-down Fridays' took root (but did anyone actually wear their weekend leisurewear and trainers to their legal and financial offices, I wonder?).

The 1980s on screen

The era is well represented with vivid filmed examples of these extreme shapes. *Dynasty* (1981–89) is probably out in front in the extreme fashion stakes. It was the story of a wealthy but exceptionally dysfunctional family from Denver, Colorado. British actress Joan Collins, who joined the cast in 1981, claims privately to have designed most of her more outrageous looks herself including the wide, razor-sharp shoulders, tiny corseted waist and towering stiletto heels. Since Ms Collins is every bit as fierce as her on-screen character, Alexis Colby,

Left Design for the production of *Figaro*, set in the 1980s.

she probably did. She and her compliant designer, Youcef Aden, captured the spirit of the age so accurately that her wardrobe quickly reached the status of style icon.

Style tribes

Rumbling away in the background, extreme street fashion, from what Ted Polhemus helpfully calls 'style tribes', was beginning to take over. Punks emerged in the 1970s, but the movement spread in the 1980s and ripped jeans, leather, rubber and vinyl were often complemented by towering, coloured Mohican hairstyles. Punks' cousins, the black-clad, ashen-faced goths, attracted attention with multiple body piercings and tattoos (pain, it seems, was no object) accessorized much black leather, silver chains and heavy boots.

The 1990s

If the 1980s was an era of excess in the high end of the fashion world, then the 1990s were much more downbeat, with the tough, triangular shapes slowly collapsing into a far softer silhouette, epitomized by deconstructed unisex suits by the Italian designer Giorgio Armani and the gentle tailoring of Calvin Klein. Grunge music was inspired by hardcore punk, heavy metal, and indie rock, it is generally characterized by heavily distorted electric guitars, contrasting song dynamics, 'growling' vocals and apathetic or angst-filled lyrics. (Think of the wan-looking Sex Pistols and Kurt Cobain). The grunge aesthetic or fashion look is the polar opposite of singers such as David Bowie or Michael Jackson. Grunge musicians were noted for their unkempt appearances and rejection of theatrics. Few people over 30, or 'respectable' or those engaged in the conventional professions, or leaning to right-wing politics, would want to have anything to do with the style, and it's the faux 'unkempt' bit that concerns us here.

Talented production assistant and enthusiastic blogger, Lisa Eppich has this to say when the grunge street style, which has been charmingly described as the 'who gives a f***' attitude to almost everything, was taken up by mainstream fashion houses in the 1990s:

We have to wonder if Kurt Cobain would shudder knowing that grunge has gone haute couture. After all, this movement was born as a way to detach from an uptight society and express discomfort with the status quo, which is not exactly in line with the hefty price-tags and hand-detailing of high fashion. Flannel shirts, ripped jeans, and lacy dresses paired with combat boots are what immediately come to mind when one thinks of grunge, but today the look is all about juxtaposing luxe with low-brow, masculine and feminine, construction and deconstruction. To channel your inner Courtney Love (minus the crazy), throw a flannel shirt over your favorite ultra-femme dress and pair it with some chunky, well-worn boots, textured tights, and cinch with a wide leather belt. Sure the angst may be gone, but we'll be happy to keep grunge in fashion long after we're done smelling like teen spirit.

I thought this style would fade away like snow in April, but it has proved amazingly long lasting. Only this year I see the ubiquitous style of sad little bare legs worn with ankle boots, short skirts and leather jackets. (Interestingly the bare legs in winter bit is only seen on fashion shoots, it's far too cold in the UK not to wear leg coverings of some kind in real life.)

Grunge style has also proved a very popular alternative and edgy way of dressing productions from many periods. It's cheap, of course, and can provide a genuine wake-up-and-re-think-this shot of adrenaline to a concept that might otherwise have been a tired re-run of old ideas.

Summing up

Much of this stylistic variety is a rich source for the inventive costume designer. Plays, films or operas written at this time might well use contemporary costuming to good effect. But the recent past can also be used to update works written in all sorts of periods. The 1980s, in particular, is especially useful as the social stereotyping was in some ways quite a throwback to more rigidly structured ages, and cleverly used can be very expressive. It is a simple matter to obtain vintage sewing patterns and plenty of original garments can still be found in all the usual places, either for use as they are if they fit both actors and your colour palette, or if not, studied for pattern construction.

Left The icons of 1990s minimalism: models Kate Moss and Christy Turlington with designer Calvin Klein.

PART 5

Case studies

Case study

Above Wolfgang behaves
badly on meeting
Constanze.

Amadeus

The Old Globe, San Diego, 2011

Main cast
Wolfgang Amadeus Mozart: Jay Whittaker
Antonio Salieri: Miles Anderson
Constanze Mozart: Winslow Corbett
Venticelli: Georgia Hatzis and Ryman Sneed

Peter Shaffer's stage play *Amadeus* (1979) is a variant of Alexander Pushkin's play *Mozart i Salieri* (1830), in which the composer Antonio Salieri recognizes the genius of Wolfgang Amadeus Mozart but poisons him out of pride and envy. The story is set in Vienna during the latter half of the eighteenth century.

The story

Pushkin's 'little tragedy', as he called it, is very brief. The story, reduced to the interaction between the two lead characters, is blatantly the stuff of fiction. As court composer, Salieri enjoys a high social position and a life of chaste dedication to his muse. Secretly, he is jealous of Mozart because he recognizes the superior quality of his music. His anger is fuelled by what he sees as the disreputable character of the younger man.

Salieri invites Mozart to dinner, planning to kill him. Mozart is haunted by an incident in which a masked stranger commissioned a requiem, ostensibly for his master; Mozart, however, has become convinced that it will be his own requiem. He then recalls *Tarare*, Salieri's collaboration with Pierre Beaumarchais, and asks if it could be true that Beaumarchais once poisoned someone, for genius and criminality are surely incompatible. Salieri then surreptitiously pours poison into Mozart's drink.

Shaffer's *Amadeus*

Shaffer's play is far more complex. We first meet Salieri as an old man, having long outlived his fame and obsessed, in his increasing dementia, with the idea that he poisoned Mozart. Speaking directly to the audience, he promises to explain himself. The action then flashes back to 1781, when Salieri was about to meet Mozart in person, having heard much of both him and his music. He adores Mozart's compositions, and is thrilled at the chance to meet Mozart in person. When the meeting takes place, however, he is appalled by the young man, thinking him to be a foul-mouthed popinjay completely at odds with the grace and charm of his compositions.

Below left Mozart plays harpsichord to the assembled Viennese court.

Below Drawing for Mozart in Act One, with sample colour swatches.

von Strack   Mozart   Joseph   van Sweiten   Bono   Orsini-Rosenber

Salieri

Salieri cannot reconcile Mozart's loutish behaviour with his apparently God-given genius. After hearing the slow movement of the *Grand Partita*, which moves him to tears, at a party where Wolfgang is behaving particularly disgracefully, he renounces God and vows to do everything in his power to destroy Mozart as a way of getting back at his creator. Throughout much of the rest of the play, Salieri masquerades as Mozart's ally while doing his utmost to destroy his reputation and success.

The play ends with Salieri cutting his throat in a last attempt to be famous, leaving a confession of having murdered Mozart with arsenic. He survives, however, and his confession is disbelieved by all, leaving him to wallow once again in furious mediocrity.

A costuming opportunity

The play does none of the characters any favours, Salieri least of all, and it is important to treat it as a work of fiction but with names you happen to have heard of. I had to keep stopping myself from leaping to the defence of nearly everyone involved as my sense of historical fair play became ever more outraged! However, it is a superbly constructed piece of theatre and gives the audience an evening of exceptional drama. And it is a once-in-a-lifetime, over-the-top showpiece for the costume designer and great fun to do!

Opposite Colour scheme for the Viennese court. Pencil drawings coloured and annotated in Photoshop.

Below Sketches for the two Venticelli and the 'whispering chorus'.

Costume scheme

Amadeus is a fantasy memory play, about real people in a specific time frame, so obviously there has to be a high level of period accuracy. Because the eighteenth-century part of the play takes place in what Shaffer describes as a 'golden glow', this indicated a palette of pinks and golds, which was, I'm pleased to say, very effective. Also, one seldom gets a chance to do those huge corseted frocks with full-on panniers, 1.5m (5ft) wide, and towering wigs – with 60cm (2ft) of ostrich feathers on top, just in case they didn't look big enough. Nowadays the fashion is to do eighteenth-century plays and operas in modern – or at least twentieth-century – dress, lest complex costumes 'get in the way'. Also, they are extremely expensive and difficult to make, requiring a level of period expertise on the part of the cutters/drapers that is seldom available.

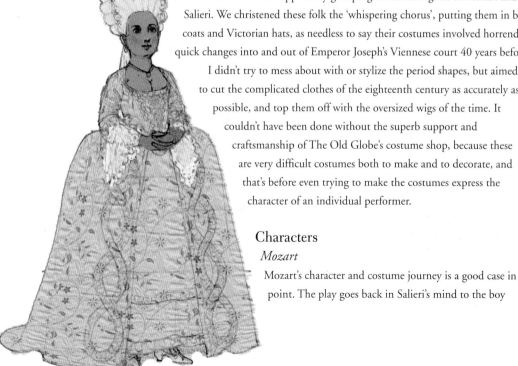

Research and references

Research is unavoidable for this play. Contemporary portraits exist of almost all the characters, so my job seemed to be to synthesize the historical images with the actors who had been cast. All the eighteenth-century episodes essentially take place in Salieri's head; thus to take Shaffer literally about the 'glow of memory' and to make all the costumes in shades of gold would achieve this quality by actually making them glow in the lighting, which featured footlights and candles.

Fabrics and wigs

We were greatly aided by a benefactor of The Old Globe, who loved the theatre and wanted to make a donation in kind. He owned a fabric shop near the Mexican border and contributed much of the rich-looking and very expensive silk brocade to the production. He specialized in exotic French and Italian party fabrics, which were ideal for us. The show must have benefitted to the tune of around $14,000-worth of unique textiles – such a gift doesn't happen very often.

The main costume design challenge was to create the outrageous glamour of the Viennese court with our comparatively modest means. We know from history books that appearances were extremely important, even if you were living on the breadline. Even when Mozart was deeply in debt and writing begging letters to his fellow Masons, he apparently still sent his lace cuffs out to be laundered and starched. So I tried to make the court costumes as showy as possible, to contrast with the increasingly grubby desolation of the Mozarts' home life. As Wolfgang and Constanze's clothes became ever more shabby, Salieri, his wife and his opera singer mistress wore correspondingly richer garments.

Amadeus begins and ends in the 1820s, at the end of Salieri's life, with the citizens of Vienna apparently gossiping about the legend of Mozart and Salieri. We christened these folk the 'whispering chorus', putting them in black coats and Victorian hats, as needless to say their costumes involved horrendous quick changes into and out of Emperor Joseph's Viennese court 40 years before. I didn't try to mess about with or stylize the period shapes, but aimed to cut the complicated clothes of the eighteenth century as accurately as possible, and top them off with the oversized wigs of the time. It couldn't have been done without the superb support and craftsmanship of The Old Globe's costume shop, because these are very difficult costumes both to make and to decorate, and that's before even trying to make the costumes express the character of an individual performer.

Characters

Mozart

Mozart's character and costume journey is a good case in point. The play goes back in Salieri's mind to the boy

Above One of the few authenticated portraits of Mozart, painted in 1819, after his death, by Barbara Kraft. This portrait provided a great reference when embarking on the costume design.

Right Drawing for Signora Salieri.

wonder's first explosive arrival at the stuffy Austrian court in 1781 and the flashbacks continue until Mozart's death, aged 35, in 1791. Jay Whittaker played Mozart with great panache and sensitivity, but he wasn't 25, therefore one of the first decisions was to modify a period wig. The grey powdered wig of the portraits, with its hard front and rigid curls, was very ageing, so after much experimentation we settled on what was essentially the eighteenth-century version of Harpo Marx's bubbly blonde hairdo, which immediately did the trick.

His first coat was in bright red and gold brocade, which looked great and provided the punchy highlight of the golden colour scheme. Coat shapes for men were actually becoming narrower by the 1780s, but somehow the fuller skirt and more defined waist of twenty years, earlier had the effect of creating a more childish silhouette and seemed to be a liberty worth taking. As the character begins to disintegrate, the first change was to give him a natural brown wig, then his clothes just got plainer with no gold, and then progressively shabbier, ending up with Jay huddled under an old rug in an effort to keep warm in his freezing apartment.

Salieri

With Salieri, the particular problem was that Miles Anderson almost never left the stage for long enough to do a complete change. He therefore had to wear his eighteenth-century clothes under his 1820s dressing gown and smoking hat. To Miles's relief, we simply couldn't use a wig for the eighteenth-century scenes: there wasn't time, it just got in the way and anyway he hates wearing them! We arranged for Salieri's valet and cook to help him with his coat and remove the dressing gown, and performs the same business at the end when he had to revert to the 1820s and pre-set the throat-cutting cravat and blood-bags.

Above left Mozart conducts in Act Two.

Above Constanze Mozart tries to sell her husband's scores to the lecherous Saleiri.

Shaffer produces another *coup de théâtre* when he makes Salieri visit the dying Mozart, disguised in a cloak and mask. In his delirium, Mozart mistakes the ghostly figure for the being who commissioned the requiem, and then gets him confused with his own father. In a distressing scene, Salieri asks for Mozart's forgiveness, but poor Wolfgang is too far gone to hear or understand what is being said.

Constanze Mozart

Shaffer imagines Constanze Mozart as a silly, feckless child who is no help to her genius husband, miscarries his child and leaves him just when she is needed, only to return as he is dying – when it is too late. In another painful scene, Constanze goes to Salieri for help, showing him the manuscripts he had asked her to bring, and Salieri attempts to seduce her. Whatever Shaffer's moral viewpoint, it is all undeniably dramatic, and Winslow Corbett was, as always, a joy to dress. If you have a character who is supposed to be a sexy, if naive 19-year-old, it does help enormously to have an actress who is only 1.5m (5ft) tall, with a tiny waist.

Her costume journey mirrored that of her husband. Adrian Noble asked that they should look like two hopelessly vulnerable, crazy children at the beginning, so I echoed Mozart's bubbly blond wig, which was, in fact, not far from Winslow's hairstyle. She is described as making her first appearance in a 'gay party dress', so I was delighted to find yellow silk with sprigs of red and green flowers for the overdress, under which was a frilled underskirt, which in turn was worn over the obligatory corset and panniered petticoat. The red silk shoes and stockings were just for fun. They looked very sweet, though, and thoroughly in character. As the Mozarts' circumstances deteriorated, so did the gaiety of her wardrobe, with little working jackets and plain brown shoes taking the place of her court finery.

Court characters

The court characters were treated as parts of the whole stage picture. I found portraits of

Opposite Saleiri remembers the past.

Below Salieri plays a welcome march for Mozart and the court.

Below right The death of Mozart.

Below left Contanze's 'gay party dress'.

Below right The Queen of the Night, based on the original design.

Opposite top The Venticelli, second costumes.

Opposite bottom Salieri and the court as spectators at the opera.

Emperor Joseph II, Count Orsini Rosenberg, Van Sweiten and the rest, and drew their costumes as lightly caricatured pencil drawings based on a point midway between the portraits and photographs of the actors that the casting department had sent to me.

I used Photoshop to make a multilayered image of all the characters in the court, and then made a coloured rendering which provided the master plan when it came to choosing the many fabrics involved. (Interestingly, the blue that Peter Shaffer suggested for Salieri looked very weak when we got it on stage, so his coat was replaced with a hurriedly made black version during the previews.) A similar composite rendering was done for the court ladies, which I adapted from the drawing of the put-upon Mrs Salieri.

Venticelli

Shaffer uses the device of a pair of characters, who nowadays would be gossip columnists or paparazzi, to keep both Salieri and the audience up to speed with the events of the court and his victims. They are written as men, but there are so few women in the play that I suggested that we switch the gender of these Venticelli, or 'little winds', as they are called. It worked very well, and enabled me to define the changing fashions from 1781 to 1795 through the shape of their dresses in a way that wasn't possible with the rest of the court, for reasons of practicality and expense. They were nosy women, and to my delight we were able to express this literally by using pointed nose extensions. It was amazing what a difference that 0.6cm (¼in) of putty made!

Opera excerpt characters

The other major element was the stage costumes needed for the excerpts from Abduction from the *Seraglio* and *The Marriage of Figaro*. The soprano in the former is a pupil of Salieri called Katherina Cavalieri who, Shaffer suggests, had a fling with Mozart. In revenge, Salieri makes her his mistress, converts her to his sugar addiction and makes her a huge star, in both senses of the term. Original costume designs do exist for those first productions, so I was able to use them as a point of departure. They were even more over the top than normal court wear, if that is possible.

Chorus

The principal cast is supported by a chorus of Viennese citizens, courtiers, servants and audiences, both grand and humble. We were mostly able to fit these characters from stock altered to fit and 'rigged' for the quick changes, of which there were many.

Overall look

The whole production of *Amadeus* came together very well. The lovely and adaptable set by Ralph Funicello was based around a movable false proscenium and lit, as if by myriad candles, by Alan Burrett. It was a textbook example of traditional period costume design done in the grand manner.

Case study

A Midsummer Night's Dream

The Old Globe, San Diego, 2013

Cast
Oberon/Theseus: Jay Whittaker
Titania/Hippolyta: Krystal Lucas
Bottom: Miles Anderson

A Midsummer Night's Dream is often the first Shakespeare play that anyone sees, with very good reason: it is approachable, funny, romantic, quite short and has fairies in it. What's not to love? Added to all that, it is almost entirely set in a forest, so no wonder it is a staple play of all outdoor theatres. I was delighted to find that it was one of the three plays chosen for our final season at The Old Globe Shakespeare Festival in San Diego in 2013 (which took place in the outdoor Lowell Davies Festival Theatre, Balboa Park), and even more delighted to find that the director was the enormously experienced Shakespearean director, Ian Talbot, who had been the director of the Regent's Park Open Air Theatre in London for eighteen years. From our first meetings in January 2013, it was clear that we were on the same wavelength and that our collaboration promised to be very enjoyable.

The story

Theseus, Duke of Athens, is preparing for his marriage to Hippolyta, Queen of the Amazons. Egeus, an Athenian nobleman, storms into the court with his daughter, Hermia, followed by two young men, Demetrius and Lysander. Egeus wishes Hermia to marry Demetrius (who loves Hermia), but Hermia is in love with Lysander and refuses to comply. Egeus asks for the full penalty of law (death or banishment to a convent) to fall on Hermia's head if she flouts her father's will. So Hermia and Lysander plan to escape and marry outside the city limits. Hermia can't stop herself blurting out the plan to her best friend Helena, who still loves Demetrius even though he jilted her after meeting Hermia. Hoping to regain his love, Helena tells Demetrius of the elopement. Demetrius thunders into the woods after his intended bride and her lover; Helena follows him.

Below Helena and Hermia's wedding garments, to be made in sweet pea-coloured Indian silks.

In these same woods are two very different groups of characters. The first is a band of fairies, led by Oberon, the fairy king, and Titania, his queen. They are quarrelling over a young Indian boy rescued by Titania after the death of his mother; Oberon wants the boy to use as a henchman, but Titania refuses. Seeking revenge, Oberon sends his servant, Puck, to acquire a magical flower, the juice of which can be spread over a sleeping person's eyelids to make that person fall in love with the first living thing he or she sees upon waking.

Puck obtains the flower, and Oberon tells him of his plan to spread its juice on the sleeping Titania's eyelids. Having seen Demetrius act cruelly towards Helena, he orders Puck to spread some of the juice on the eyelids of the young Athenian. Needless to say, Puck gets the wrong man and both boys forsake Hermia and fall for Helena, which causes the most tremendous quarrel.

The second group is a band of Athenian craftsmen, known as 'The Mechanicals', who hope to perform a play during the wedding festivities of the duke and his bride. When they retire to the forest to rehearse, the mischievous Puck changes Bottom the Weaver's head into the head of an ass. When Titania wakes, the first 'creature' she sees is Bottom. She is immediately entranced by him, to Bottom's comical amazement. Oberon abducts the Indian boy while Titania is in no state to resist, before awakening his bemused queen.

Out hunting early the following morning, Theseus and Hippolyta discover the two pairs of sleeping lovers in the forest, now in love with the right partners, and they all go back to Athens to be married. The three bridal couples then watch The Mechanicals perform the

increasingly demented play of *Pyramus and Thisbe*. Afterwards, the fairies emerge to bless the sleeping couples with a protective charm for themselves and their future children. Only Puck remains, to ask the audience to remember the play as though it had all been a dream.

Costume scheme

As is often the case with the *Dream*, the fairy characters seem to come first: get them right and the humans are easily adaptable to fit. We started with a list of the qualities we didn't want the fairies to have, such as being twee, sweetly pretty, spineless, over-romantic, or wearing ballet tutus, wings and so forth. On the other hand, neither were they just inadequate humans or gnomic aliens, and we didn't have CGI technology to help us out, as in *The Lord of the Rings* or *Harry Potter*. Ian's thoughts were that they should be somewhat malevolent, reminiscent of the Lost Boys from *Peter Pan* and, given the power that Oberon's bad temper has over the weather, nature spirits.

First references

Here are some of the references I began to explore.

- Arthur Rackham's quirky 1908 illustrations for the play. These are beautiful and mysterious, drawn in a murky palette of sepias and bleached umbers. Of course, being drawings, Rackham doesn't have to stick to a realistic human scale, but never mind.
- The costumes of the *Mad Max* films (1979 and 1981), as brilliantly imagined by the Australian production designer Norma Moriceau. Her look for the films, which I think is terrific, is described as 'post-apocalyptic leather-fetish biker-warrior'.
- The litter pickers (often called New Age travellers) who are employed by the big music festivals to clear up and recycle the mountains of trash. (The Glastonbury festival takes ten days to clear.)
- A far-off memory of the first production of the *Dream* I ever saw, in 1960, which was designed by Lila di Nobili. The

humans were in black and white, the fairies in green with wigs that looked like thistledown. I liked the wigs.

Choosing the period

Ian wanted to set the humans sometime in the nineteenth century. The difficulty about setting this play in modern times is that it has to be believable that a Western father (Egeus) can threaten to kill his daughter (Hermia) if she refuses to marry the man he has chosen for her. The nineteenth century seemed to be about the latest period when this proposition could work. Costume-wise, of earlier periods, sixteenth-century Elizabethan clothes, with their balloon breeches and farthingales, seemed too structured and restrictive, as were those of the seventeenth and eighteenth centuries. I didn't want mid-nineteenth-century crinolines for the same reason.

Oberon tells Puck that he will recognize the lovers by 'the Athenian garments he hath on', so I looked at the paintings of Lawrence Alma Tadema, who specialized in highly romanticized images of beautiful people lolling about in the Grecian countryside in a series of beautiful dresses – Athenian enough for me.

If anyone asked or wanted to know a date for patterns to look at, I said around 1900. Using the nineteenth century in this relaxed, not to say cavalier, way meant that we could put Theseus and Demetrius in the exceedingly smart red and black military uniforms I had done for a production of *As You Like It* at The Old Globe a couple of years previously, which was set in 1820, and using red meant that we could give the Windsor footmen's liveries from *The Madness of George III* (eighteenth century, but formal footman's liveries haven't changed) another outing. Reuse not only helps the budget, but reduces a costume shop's work time.

As for third group, The Mechanicals, who consist of well-loved characters such as Bottom the Weaver, Flute the Bellows Mender, Peter Quince et al., 'hard-handed men of Athens who never laboured with their brains until now', you always hope that they can be dressed mostly from stock for a couple of reasons: firstly the budget, but also because well-used clothes look so much better.

Drawing

Towards the end of January 2013 I began to draw, beginning with Oberon and Titania, who are by far the most difficult characters to get right. When designing three shows at once, as I was here (at the time, I was working as the House Designer for the Shakespeare Festival, which involved designing the costumes for three different shows each season – all at the same time), I try to make the drawings in different styles, mostly to emphasize the individuality of the world of the play, but also to keep the plays un-muddled in my head.

Given the woodland setting, I decided to explore drawing on my iPad using an app called SketchBook Pro that I had bought some months

Above Demetrius in uniform, Act One.

Left Moth's punkish costume, drawn on the iPad.

Opposite top Arthur Rackham's fairy illustrations.

Opposite bottom Further inspiration came from the *Mad Max* films.

Opposite Costumes
designs developed and
coloured on the iPad.

Below Theseus and
Hippolyta in their
wedding attire.

before. Like Photoshop, you can work in layers, but unlike that program you can, with practice and a good-quality stylus, draw very accurately straight onto the screen using the many brushes, textures and colour combinations. It's neither easy nor particularly quick, but I liked the results very much, they were very easy to transmit to San Diego via Dropbox or e-mail, and printed out on art paper, no one could tell how they had been done – which pleased me! So I imported atmospheric forest photographs from my library to act as backgrounds, and then drew the costume onto the second layer.

Fairies

Certain images began to form – the wild hair, for instance, arrived quite quickly. From work we had done on the goddess puppets for *The Tempest* a couple of years before, I knew we could use a mixture of yak, human hair and shredded nylon crin to create the windswept thistledown look. As for the fairies' feet, I had been very taken with the five-toed running shoes we had used for Ariel in the same *Tempest* production, which made it look as if the actor was barefoot but would actually protect feet from the splinter-prone festival stage. Also, I was pleased with the idea that it would make the fairies look a bit like hobbits, with their enlarged feet, and less human.

Humans

Then came ideas for the humans, starting with the pretty Grecian-style dresses and formal menswear for the lovers in the first scene in Theseus's palace, a few ideas for the progressively more deconstructed garments for the forest, and some thoughts for the wedding at the end.

I decided to leave the detailed decisions about the forest stuff until rehearsals, as I didn't know how extreme Ian's thoughts were (very physical and athletic, as it turned out). I decided that Hippolyta was powerful enough to impose her Amazonian ideas on her husband and the lovers at the end, so rather than conforming to boring Western evening dress, I sketched costumes that involved harem pants and silk embroidered coats in sweet pea colours – on paper this time.

The play within a play of *Pyramus and Thisbe*, where The Mechanicals dress up in homemade costumes and Bottom's head is turned into that of an ass, includes probably the most famous and discussed props in Shakespeare. I decided to leave definite decisions until I could have a discussion with the actors: they had to get on stage and perform, after all, and their considered input would be helpful.

San Diego

On 9 April 2013, I flew to San Diego. We had two weeks before the actors arrived in which to buy fabrics and for the cutters to work on patterns before all the fittings started, and for me to finish the drawings.

My first task, when at least partially recovered from the jet lag, was

Lion

Flute as Thisbe

Fairy

Cobweb

to explain my ideas for the season's plays to the costume shop. At this stage in a production, it is essential that everyone involved is fully engaged with the process and made aware of the sort of world I am trying to create (it's quite hard not to sound like a candidate for 'Pseuds' Corner' in *Private Eye* here). One must describe the imagined world in inspiring terms, while at the same time trying to be practical. This is where being able to draw clearly and reasonably entertainingly comes in very handy, as it will do on the first day of rehearsal, when members of the production team are expected to do a 'show and tell' for the actors and stage management.

Characters

The actors playing Oberon and Titania were doubling as Theseus and Hippolyta. As well as the need for vivid characterization, there were some extremely tricky quick changes to negotiate for them both.

Oberon / Theseus

Jay Whittaker, our Oberon/Theseus, was well known to The Old Globe, having played a wide variety of roles including Mozart in *Amadeus*, Oliver in *As You Like It* and, the previous year, *Richard III*. I thought he would be brilliant as Oberon, as indeed he was. Oberon has many qualities, not all of them attractive: he is jealous, vengeful and sulky as well as graceful, passionate and very sexy. I kept thinking of black-patched leather and chains for his first scenes – rather like Richard III with fairy feet and more hair. Oddly enough, it is often the leading characters who end up in the simplest costumes; you let the secondary characters, such as the chorus of fairies, have all the details. It seems to work for me.

As Theseus, we wanted to make as big a contrast as possible to the flighty Oberon, so

Below Demetrius with Helena and Hermia on stage.

the obvious answer was to dress him in rigidly correct military uniform, followed by classic British riding clothes complete with top hat, moustache and riding crop. This all slotted into place when the idea of Jay speaking his lines like Prince Charles was floated. The whole characterization immediately worked brilliantly, being both touching and funny, as did the Jungian idea that his two characters were each other's shadow.

Titania / Hippolyta

I then applied the same thought process to the very beautiful Krystal Lucas as Hippolyta/ Titania. Her first dress was inspired by nineteenth-century aristocratic national dress from the Benaki Museum in Athens. It had to be red to stand its ground with the uniforms, so I was pleased to find a lavishly gold-embroidered red silk sari in an Indian store just outside San Diego, which was also the source of all the wedding garment fabrics. The point of departure for Hippolyta's hunting costume came from an ancient piece of pottery that purported to be Amazonian dress. Somehow I didn't see her riding side-saddle in a demure black habit.

Bottom

As the fittings progressed, we were able to 'grow' the costumes to suit the actors and the demands of the play. For a start, Miles Anderson as Bottom initially wanted his face covered, so that what the audience was aware of was the grotesque ass's head. He soon found this far too restricting, and a beautiful cane frame with woolly ears was built by Erin Leah, the head of crafts. But eventually even this proved too distracting, as the eye was drawn to the mask instead of the various panic-stricken expressions on Miles's face, so we fell back on the solution of the ears and specially made large donkey teeth.

Fairies

Everyone had great fun with the construction of the fairies' costumes. Every piece of fabric was processed in some way – patch-dyed, shredded like a spider's web, or turned into feathers. Strange bits of knitting were attacked with blowtorches and cheese graters; hair and neck

Above left The Lion's socks and mane.

Above right The wigs for the fairies.

Titania - Blessing

ornaments were constructed from bits of leather, glass and wire. The fairies' shoes were treated to look like feet, and stripy socks recycled from the cut-off arms of ancient sweaters fished out from boxes in the basement under the stage. These costumes were absurdly labour-intensive but so effective and popular that no one seemed to mind.

Mechanicals

The makeshift costumes for *Pyramus and Thisbe* were coming along nicely. I did quick drawings in the end: it just saves time to have a clear image. My theory was that The Mechanicals might not have been over-bright or polished at acting, but they were very good craftsmen, so I thought of their available talents and used them to inform the construction of their costumes. After all, Snug the Joiner and Quince the Carpenter could have dealt with the woodwork, Flute the Bellows Mender could have worked with leather, and Snout the Tinker could presumably have found and mended anything (we gave him a helmet made from a bread tin). Don Carrier was developing a bossy and ever so slightly camp persona as Starveling the Tailor, and he was obviously a fine costumier, so he could have made Flute's frock as well as his own.

Bottom had, of course, been absent during the main making period doing unmentionable things with Titania, but I imagined that his friends would have rallied round with his beer barrel armour, wooden sword and saucepan helmet.

Fairy world finale

The one final problem to be solved was how to present the fairy world for the finale. Puck, in the splendid form of Lucas Hall, rises slowly through a trapdoor with a broom to clear the way for the wedding blessing that will be delivered by Oberon, Titania and all the fairies. (Puck's speech needs to cover the hectic 50-second quick change that is going on under the stage.)

I had originally thought that the woodland nature spirit aspect of the fairies would become most clear for the ending of the play, but I began to feel that the green, woodsy capes and flower headdresses I had drawn belonged far too much to the daytime, so I decided on white garments instead. Somehow it made sense of the occasion and all the fairy lights. So Oberon had paler, extremely tight trousers and a huge transparent cape in layers of cream and stone that framed Jay's spectacular bare chest, which Alan Burrett somehow lit to look like carved alabaster. Titania had a full, strapless dress appliquéd with moonlit hills and clouds, which seemed lit from within. I don't often gasp with delight at my own costumes, but in front of the towering, magically lit trees of Balboa Park, the effect was truly amazing.

Opposite Titania in her striking costume, enchanced by the stage lighting.

Below Oberon in his black rock star outfit.

Case study

Above Amelia and Adorno declare their love.

Simon Boccanegra

The Royal Opera House, London, 1997

Main Cast
Adorno: Plácido Domingo
Boccanegra: Sergei Leiferkus
Amelia: Kallen Esperian
Fiesco: Jaakko Ryhänen

I could have chosen a number of more recent opera productions for this third case study, but the grand craziness of this production, with its combination of budget and political issues and the presence of a world-class opera star, still makes it of interest.

Work began in May 1997 at the Royal Opera House (ROH) in Covent Garden for what was known as *Boccanegra '57*. This was to be a rare production of the 1857 version of Verdi's *Simon Boccanegra*, which is normally performed in the 1881 version. Part of the logic and poignancy of this production was that Plácido Domingo would give one of his last performances as a tenor in the role of Adorno. Also cast were the Russian baritone Sergei Leiferkus in the title role, and the American soprano Kallen Esperian as Amelia.

Boccanegra '57 was to be the last new production before the ROH closed for two years for rebuilding. Because of this there was a great deal of uncertainty in the ROH, as at least a third of the staff were to be laid off. Morale had not been helped by the abrupt resignation of Genista McIntosh as chief executive, in despair about the administrative chaos left by the previous regime. In fact, the comings and goings reported in the press at the time were every bit as convoluted as the plot of *Boccanegra*.

Below Drawing for Adorno in Act One.

The story

The opera is set in Genoa in the fourteenth century, when the city was ruled by opposing groups of patricians and plebeians. The conflict is personified in Jacopo Fiesco, a city father, and Simon Boccanegra, a famous and popular corsair (a sort of pirate, only more romantic) who, prior to the opera, has impregnated Fiesco's daughter, Maria. Imprisoned, Maria dies giving birth to a daughter, Amelia, who is adopted by the Grimaldi (Fiesco's family name) and knows nothing of her parentage.

On his election as Doge, Boccanegra banishes Fiesco. In Act Two, as an uprising led by Fiesco approaches the city, Boccanegra is poisoned by Paolo, who wants to marry Amelia Grimaldi for political reasons; however, she is in love with Adorno, the tenor. Adorno charges in, having been fired up by Paulo to believe that his beloved is having an affair with Boccanegra, whom we have just found out is actually Amelia's father.

Adorno then suppresses the insurrection on the now much weakened Boccanegra's behalf. Fiesco and the dying Boccanegra come face to face just before Amelia and Adorno's wedding feast. They are reconciled and Boccanegra reveals to everyone the identity of Amelia's mother, Fiesco's daughter Maria. I hope that's clear!

Budget
The costume budget was £45,000. This sounds like a lot of money until you see what it had to cover. There were six principals who required three costumes each, as the action covered a timespan of twenty years. The original budget

was drawn up on the basis of a chorus of 50, but conductor Mark Elder expanded it to 66, all of whom required two, sometimes three costumes. Additionally, there were eleven actors and six dancers. So we rapidly reached 185 costumes and counting.

Each principal's costume could not possibly cost less than £1,000, so that left only about £150 per costume for the remainder. When you bear in mind that a tailored frock coat cost at least £800 at 1997 prices, and a plain nineteenth-century dress £1,000–£1,500, you can see how tight things were. In normal circumstances, that wouldn't be quite as bad as it appears, since there is a certain amount of 'below-the-line' assistance (that is, when things are made by the in-house wardrobe department and its normal practice is to charge only the cost of the fabrics to the show's budget while the wages are part of the fixed overheads). But the ROH Wardrobe decided that only Plácido Domingo's and Kallen Esperian's costumes were to be made in house. Everything else would therefore have to be made by freelance costume-makers, so all their fees would have to come directly out of the budget.

A further headache was that we were instructed to create a production that could be revived. This meant that we couldn't save money by hiring the costumes (not that you ever can hire that much for opera singers, as they tend to come in significantly larger sizes than most actors – upon whom the stock sizes of the various hire companies are based). So we had to rely on the ROH's stock of costumes from 'dead' shows, with the exception of some *Traviata* crinoline frames that we were allowed to borrow. The costume 'mortuary' was conveniently situated in a remote Welsh valley. The only bit of good news is was that we had Allan Watkins as costume supervisor, with whom I've worked at Stratford and elsewhere. He really is the tops, and if anyone can bring a project in on time and on budget it'll be him.

Costume scheme

Choosing the period

All these limitations had the effect of freezing my imagination, and so in the earlier part of the year I had great difficulty in actually getting down to designing the costumes. Ian Judge (the director), John Gunter (the set designer) and I took a long time to settle on the best period in which to set it. Ian was emphatically against the fifteenth century, as the costumes of the period consist of men in tights, floor-length scalloped sleeves

and huge, upside-down bucket hats. Though I quite like the sleeves, I do rather agree about the hats and the tights. We all felt that modern costumes weren't appropriate – which left us with the period of composition, 1857, as the main workable alternative. But a further problem existed for me: knowing the kind of powerful emblematic statements John was planning for the sets, I felt that realistic nineteenth-century costumes would look too frail and fussy. After some dithering, I remembered an Italian painting by Pellizza representing the Risorgimento (the unification of Italy, of which Verdi was a passionate supporter), which depicts a large crowd of working men and women wearing simple nineteenth-century clothes, in shades of raw and burnt sienna, striding purposefully forward into a beautiful light. It seemed to have just the right feel about it, so I did a few sketches and showed them to Ian with a copy of the painting. He was immediately enthusiastic, and so our central idea or concept rapidly emerged as a Verdi-esque statement featuring Garibaldi, his red shirt brigade and a revolting populace.

Above The populace in matching terracotta.

Above left The citizens make for a strking appearance on stage.

Colour scheme

I was careful to colour in the sketches as Ian, in common with many directors, sometimes finds it difficult to 'see' pencil drawings, and what emerged was a carefully colour-coded scheme, which was beginning to look very good. In such a complex plot, it's essential to ensure that colours work as an identifying feature, like a football team's jerseys. Our townspeople and peasants were to be in shades of terracotta, working through Venetian red and purple to deep blue for the upper classes. Boccanegra himself retained a sumptuous deep red, not just to remind us of his plebeian origins but also because the Doges traditionally dressed from head to toe in

red, like Catholic cardinals. Some colour archetypes are too ingrained in the psyche
to be ignored.

From slaves to captives

Alan called me in early May to discuss scheduling. He said that there was a miserable
atmosphere in the theatre because one of the choristers had just thrown herself under a train.
The ROH had been laying off staff in preparation for the shutdown, and she had just received
her notice. Even more tragically, she was the mother of a young child.

I called Ian, who was directing *Così fan tutte* at Garsington Opera, to find out his
thoughts on the 'prisoners' (the stage directions indicate that a boatload of burly African
slaves are unloaded in Genoa, who are persuaded to perform an exotic ethnic dance – Verdian
tambourines and all). Unfortunately, our boatload consisted of only three couples of fragile-
looking dancers!

It was decided to bypass the political minefield by calling them 'captives'. I was rather
hoping that the captives could be proud trophies, the unspoiled spoils of war as it were, but Ian
wanted them to look sad and lonely in contrast to the gung-ho jingoism of the chorus. Perhaps
there was a way of combining these ideas – proud but sad, exotic and lonely, politically correct
and disturbingly imperialistic? I decided to trawl through Max Tilke's *Costume Patterns and
Designs* for a basic shape and then see what could be done with bleach to achieve a faded, sad
exoticism. I was hoping that what emerged would be a shining example of the real design
process, i.e. the designer has one idea, the director an apparently opposing one, so rather
than agreeing to a spineless compromise, a third idea is grown from the best bits of the
two original viewpoints. And in theory everybody is happy…

Rehearsals

On the first day of the rehearsals, Ian said that he felt that Boccanegra needed a
special robe to die in. I failed to pack for London until the last minute, and as
a result I forgot the new drawings and had to go to Cornelissen's art shop and
buy paper, gold ink and a set of calligraphy pens to redraw the forgotten
sketches. In fact, my redone Boccanegra-as-Doge was a distinct improvement
on my first sketch.

The velvet of Boccanegra's 'dying robe' was to be dyed to the colour of brown
paper, with a deep border dipped and shadowed in a dark blood red. I had a
meeting with the dye room about this, and wrote blocks of medieval-looking
letters interspersed with boldly scripted initials on the red bits with the newly
purchased black ink, picking out the capital letters in gold.

Ian Judge gave an excellent introductory team talk to everyone. I could
see well over a hundred people in the room before losing count. John

Gunter's model of the set was extremely striking and although Ian was initially rather taken aback at suddenly seeing my new drawings, he liked them a lot and gave a very encouraging introduction explaining the ideas behind the costume designs – which always makes it much easier to deal with the performers in the fittings, when they start trying to object to things or wanting to bring in ideas of their own.

As the whole enormous opera had only two weeks' rehearsal time, the scheduling of everything was critical. Even worse, Domingo was not able to be in London for the first week. A rumour that Domingo might cancel began flying around. I didn't know if it was true, or just because he was due in on Friday the 13th. Domingo might not have been the entire reason that we were doing the 1857 version, but he was certainly the reason why the entire run was already sold out!

Then Domingo got a cold and cancelled a recital in Berlin. Everyone was on tenterhooks trying to decipher what this meant. It was rather like the situation in a great eighteenth-century house where everyone below stairs is trying to guess when, or if, their lord and master will arrive.

Boccanegra himself was played by Sergei Leiferkus, whom I had costumed in 1990 in the title role in *Prince Igor,* or 'Prince Ego', as my son named it. He came directly from the 'authentic' nineteenth-century Russian tradition, and as far as he was concerned, that was the only way to do it. He exhibited little willingness to engage with or to trust the overall design concept. He came round by the time we got on stage, when he could see how good he looked.

Above left In the fitting room. Amelia's hand-stencilled velveteen coat.

Above right Amelia wears the coat on stage.

Fitting day

On fitting day, I got to the ROH at about 1p.m. to find the place abuzz. Domingo's fitting was at 3 o'clock. At five past three, his assistant arrived to say that Plácido was partaking of coffee. Although one part of me thought it absurd to get excited about meeting yet another performer, I found myself anticipating the encounter keenly. After all, it's not every day that you're in the same room as a living legend. Twenty minutes later, someone heard the lift doors down below and rushed into the fitting room to let us know that He was coming. Everyone's blasé mask slipped badly for a few minutes, but professionalism won out and they quickly calmed down.

A few moments later, the lift doors clanked and in swept the great man himself surrounded by his entourage – Signora Domingo and the assistant, followed by his personal répétiteur bearing the score. Mercifully, the fitting went extremely well. Plácido liked everything, looked wonderful and said that all the clothes were comfortable. The house tailor had done a great job. More importantly, Signora Martha Domingo approved (we had heard that she is the final arbiter, and her disapproval could render a designer's best efforts useless).

After discussion, we all felt that the purple suede purchased for the second coat would be less perfect than an elegant linen one – whose colour I suggested should match a lovely scarf that Signora D. had about her neck. A happy marriage of diplomacy and aesthetics, perhaps.

Unrest and politics

The curse of the Scottish Play struck again. The premiere of a new production of *Macbeth*, which was to precede ours, was cancelled. It was said that no one had checked sufficiently carefully to see if those stage staff still in possession of their jobs could strike *Boccanegra* to build *Macbeth* in the available time. Moreover, there was apparently nobody from senior management in the theatre when they were doing the fit-up on the Sunday to take emergency executive decisions. So all that work and all those hundreds of thousands of pounds were poured down the drain. The sets and costumes were now to be stored for four years. Anthony Ward, the designer, wouldn't let the costumes be seen without the set, and some of the soloists said they were too angry to do concert performances – so that appeared to be that. Except, of course, that it wasn't! When I received the next week's costume calls, a *Macbeth* costume change rehearsal was scheduled. Of course we were all anxious to see if there would be a knock-on effect, where our production also became a pawn in ROH politics.

At the last chorus costume rehearsal, I watched to be certain that the costumes would be capable of doing what the action demanded, so avoiding too many nasty shocks at the piano dress rehearsal on the following Monday, when there would be nearly 100 people on stage and little chance of adjusting anything major.

First night

I'm not usually tremendously excited by first nights. I get my adrenaline rush from the relief of getting through the technical dress rehearsals; the public (or general) dress rehearsal is the really nerve-wracking bit. Premieres are sometimes a bit of an anticlimax for designers. You've seen that it all works, and your part in it is over. Now it's completely up to the performers and the stage staff. But it was impossible not to have a certain sense of anticipation, because Domingo just is such a wonderful performer. Off stage he is slightly stooped, but once he gets on stage, he really does shed the years. Perhaps not 30 years, but a very good 25!

Below Designs for Amelia's waiting women.

Postscript

Above All is revealed.
Adorno, Boccanegra and
the ROH chorus.

In 2008 this production was revived in the more conventional 1881 version, with the famous courtroom scene, but there were a few problems. I quote from interviews with the conductor, Sir John Eliot Gardiner, at the time:

> *Hardly a week seems to have gone by recently without a press release being sent out by the Royal Opera about another casting change for this* Boccanegra *(the latest has just announced that Orlin Anastassov, out of the first few performances through illness, won't now return to the production at all). [It looked more like the sulks to us …] It began back in January with the withdrawal of Nina Stemme, who was to have made her debut as Amelia. We are very lucky to now have Anja Harteros in the part.*

Harteros certainly grabbed attention in her Royal Opera House debut, with a stunning performance as Amelia, but it wasn't all plain sailing. 'I had two piano rehearsals with her and the next time I saw her was at the dress rehearsal', Gardiner said. Such is the frantic lifestyle of jet-setting musicians that Anja had a previous commitment in Madrid. 'But she is so good,' he added, 'that she fitted in very quickly.'

Another replacement was Italian bass Feruccio Furlanetto, who stood in as Fiesco for the indisposed Anastassov and would now do most of the remaining performances. Gardiner described him as 'luxury casting'. He was rehearsing for Philip II in the forthcoming *Don Carlos*

and 'wandered into rehearsal one day so we grabbed him'. With no rehearsal time, he too slipped seamlessly into the production and Gardiner said it was now as though they had rehearsed together for a full three weeks.

However, neither singer 'fitted seamlessly' into their predecessor's costume, and everything except for the sweeping robes had to be remade. This is when a top-class, in-house costume shop comes into its own. The other problem was that the entire men's chorus, all 48 of them, had to have new senator's robes for the reinstated courtroom scene, involving 11m (12yd) of cloth each. Plus hats. That was approximately 457m (500yd) of material and there was hardly any money left. We were fortunate to find furnishing damask in dark red and dark blue, our two colours, in a dusty warehouse somewhere near the North Circular (a desolate highway on the edge of London), which was actually just right for nineteenth-century legal robes and very, very cheap. A tailor with a large workroom in London's East End made them up in three basic sizes at great speed. They looked very good in the end, when seen all together and tactfully lit.

Diary of the first piano dress rehearsal

The first piano dress rehearsal has just finished. It was spread over two mornings, Monday and Wednesday, as the *Macbeth* general rehearsal was Tuesday a.m. It's been very good really. Only one remake: Leiferkus, of course – who thought his wonderful leather coat emphasized his bum. In fact the problem was that he hadn't got a proper collar or wig. So in a break, someone zoomed out to buy a shirt in Cecil Gee's sale and a necktie was found to go with a new, long-haired wig. Even as I write, another coat in needlecord with more operatic, i.e. bigger, shoulder pads is being finished off.

Oh help! Plácido has just come on stage saying that the soprano must have a wedding dress. This is true, and in a properly funded show she would have had one. We all go into a huddle with the producer after the rehearsal. To no one's surprise, money is magically found for a new frock for Kallen – what a surprise.

Anyway, I hastily sketch a new wedding gown. It'll be a quick change, so rather than make Kallen scramble into a new, tight-fitting dress, I design a great flowing coat-robe that will go on over her blue dress. We remember that there was some lovely soft sage green silk dupion with a simple printed gold pattern at Henri Bertrand's, and someone is sent in a taxi to buy 10m (11yd). Then, using the other velvet coat as a pattern, the cutter and three stitchers stay late and miraculously ... the next day a beautiful, gleaming new robe appears at the general rehearsal (traditionally this is the first dress rehearsal in front of an invited audience), with its peacock lining just picking up an echo of the blue of Amelia's main dress. Both it, and she, did look lovely.

Glossary

Armour: A mail, defensive covering worn in combat.

Ballets Russes: An itinerant ballet company based in Paris who performed between 1909 and 1929.

Berliner Ensemble: German theatre company established by playwright Bertolt Brecht in East Berlin in 1949.

Broadway: Performances presented in one of the 40 professional theatres located in the Theater District and Lincoln Center along Broadway, in the Manhattan borough of New York City.

Castrati: A type of classical male singing voice produced by castration of the singer before puberty, or it occurs in one who, due to an endocrinological condition, never reaches sexual maturity.

CGI (Computer-Generated Imagery): 3D computer graphics used for creating scenes or special effects in films and television.

Chiton: Garment worn by Greek men and women from the Archaic period to the Hellenistic period.

Corset: Supportive lingerie worn by women from the 1550s to the 1920s. Living history reenactors and historic costume enthusiasts still wear stays and corsets according to their original purpose, to give the proper shape to the figure when wearing historic fashions.

Costume: 1. Wardrobe and dress in general, or the distinctive style of dress of a particular people, class, or period. Also refers to the artistic arrangement of accessories in a picture, statue, poem, or play, appropriate to the time, place, or other circumstances represented or described, or to a style of clothing worn to portray the wearer as a character other than their regular persona at a social event such as a masquerade, a fancy dress party or a theatrical performance. **2.** A ladies' tailored skirt suit popular in the first part of the 20th century.

Cothurni: 1. A high, built-up boot or buskin worn by actors in ancient Greek and Roman tragedies, to allow characters to seem taller than their fellows. **2.** The stately tragic plays performed while wearing the said boots.

Coup de theatre: A theatrical trick or gesture, staged for dramatic effect.

Crin/horse-hair: Finely woven synthetic flat braiding used as a lightweight stiffener for underskirts and millinery.

Electronic drawing aids: Computer programmes, such as Photoshop, Autocad, Dragon Frame Animation software, Wacom tablets or drawings apps for ipads, developed to aid almost every kind of design discipline.

English Stage Company (ESC): The resident company of the Royal Court Theatre in Sloane Square, London.

Folies Bergère: A cabaret music hall, located in Paris, France. Established in 1869, the house was at the height of its fame and popularity from the 1890's Belle Époque through the 1920's Années folles.

Follies: Lavish revues, first produced in 1907 at the roof theatre Jardin de Paris.

Mask: An object normally worn on the face, typically for protection, disguise, performance or entertainment, used since antiquity for both ceremonial and practical purposes.

Masque: Festive courtly entertainment that flourished in 16th- and early 17th-century Europe.

Middle Ages: 5th to 15th centuries, from the collapse of the Western Roman Empire and merged into the Renaissance. The Middle Ages is the middle period of the three traditional divisions of Western history: Antiquity, the Medieval period, and the Modern period.

Mood board: A collage of images, text, and samples used to develop design concepts.

Music Hall, Vaudeville and Burlesque: British theatrical entertainment popular between 1850 and 1960. It involved a mixture of popular songs, comedy, speciality acts and variety entertainment.

Pantomime: A musical comedy stage production, developed in the UK and is generally performed during Christmas and New Year.

Proscenium Arch: A 'window' around the scenery and performers. Anything not intended to be seen is simply placed outside the 'window'.

Prosthetics: Using prosthetic sculpting, molding and casting techniques to create advanced cosmetic effects.

Puppets: An inanimate object or representational figure animated or manipulated by a puppeteer.

The Royal Opera House (ROH): Britain's premier opera house, in Covent Garden, London.

The Royal Shakespeare Company (RSC): A major British theatre company, based in Stratford-upon-Avon, Warwickshire, England. The core repertoire is based on the plays of William Shakespeare.

The Restoration Period: The Restoration of the English monarchy began when the English, Scottish and Irish monarchies were all restored under Charles II after the Interregnum that followed the Wars of the Three Kingdoms. The term Restoration is used to describe both the actual event by which the monarchy was restored, and the period of several years afterwards in which a new political settlement was established.

Tie-dyeing: A modern term for a set of ancient resist-dyeing techniques, consisting of folding, twisting, pleating, or crumpling fabric or a garment and binding with string or rubber bands, followed by application of dye(s).

Vacforming: A sheet of plastic is heated to a forming temperature, stretched onto a convex or into a concave single-surface mold, and forced against the mold by a vacuum (suction of air). The vacuum forming process can be used to make most product packaging and speaker casings, but in the theatre it is used for the making of masks, armour and moldings.

Vestments: Liturgical garments and articles associated primarily with the Christian religion.

Further Reading

Arnold, Janet (1985) *Patterns of Fashion: The cut and construction of clothes for men and women c.1520-1620,* Drama Books (UK) and Quite Specific Media (US)

Arnold, Janet (1977) *Patterns of Fashion 1, Englishwomen's dresses and their construction c.1660–1860, Macmillan (UK) and Quite Specific Media (US)*

Arnold, Janet (1977) Patterns of Fashion 2, Englishwomen's dresses and their construction c.1860–1940, Macmillan (UK) and Quite Specific Media (US)

Arnold, Janet (2008) *Patterns of Fashion 4: The cut and construction of linen shirts, smocks, neckwear, headwear and accessories for men and women c. 1540 – 1660,* Macmillan (UK) and Costume and Fashion Pr (US)

Ashelford, Jane (2011) *The Art of Dress: Clothes Through History 1500-1914,* National Trust Books

Bruhn, Wolfgang and Tilke, Max (2004) *A Pictorial History of Costume From Ancient Times to the Nineteenth Century: With Over 1900 Illustrated Costumes,* Dover Publications Inc.

Cosgrave, Bronwyn (2001) *The Complete History of Costume & Fashion: From Ancient Egypt to the Present Day,* Checkmark Books

Cunnington, C. Willett and Cunnington, Phillis (1992) *The History of Underclothes,* Dover Fashion and Costumes

Dars, Celestine (1979) *A Fashion Parade: The Seeberger Collection,* Blond & Briggs

Earle, Alice Morse (2007) *Two Centuries of Costume in America 1620-1820,* Dodo Press

Elgin, Kathy (2009) *Elizabethan England (Costume and Fashion Source Books)* Chelsea House Publishers

Elgin, Kathy (2009) *Medieval World (Costume and Fashion Source Books)* Chelsea House Publishers

Fernald, Mary and Shenton, Eileen (2006) *Historic Costumes and How to Make Them,* Dover Publications Inc.

Friendship, Elizabeth (2013) *Creating Historical Clothes,* Batsford

Laver, James and de la Haye, Amy (2012) *Costume and Fashion (Fifth Edition) (World of Art),* Thames & Hudson

Maclochlainn, Jason (2011) *The Victorian Tailor,* Batsford.

McEvoy, Anne (2009) *1920s and 1930s (Costume and Fashion Source Books)* Chelsea House Publishers

McEvoy, Anne (2009) *American West (Costume and Fashion Source Books)* Chelsea House Publishers

Mikhaila, Ninya, Malcom-Davies, Jane and Perry, Michael (2006) *The Tudor Tailor: Reconstructing Sixteenth-Century Dress,* Batsford

Peacock, John (2010) *The Chronicle of Western Costume: From the Ancient World to the Late Twentieth Century,* Thames & Hudson

Rooney, Anne (2009) *1950s and 1960s (Costume and Fashion Source Books)* Chelsea House Publishers

Steer, Deirdre Clancy (2009) *1980s and 1990s (Costume and Fashion Source Books)* Chelsea House Publishers

Steer, Deirdre Clancy and Baksic, Amela (2009) *Colonial America (Costume and Fashion Source Books)* Chelsea House Publishers

Taschek, Karen (2009) *Civil War (Costume and Fashion Source Books)* Chelsea House Publishers

Tetart-Vittu, Francoise (2012) *Auguste Racinet, the Costume History: 25 Years,* Taschen

Tilke, Max and Hamilton, L. (2011) *Oriental Costumes, Their Designs And Colors,* Nabu Press

Tyrrell, Anne (2010) *Classic Fashion Patterns,* Batsford

Tyrrell, Anne (2013) *Vintage Dress Patterns of the 20th Century,* Batsford

Waugh, Norah (1987) *Corsets and Crinolines,* Batsford

Waugh, Norah (1964) The Cut of Men's Clothes 1600-1900, Faber

Men-at-Arms series: Various titles published by Osprey Military

List of Suppliers

EUROPE

Angels The Costumiers
1 Garrick Road
London NW9 6AA
tel: 020 8202 2244
www.angels.uk.com

Cosprop Ltd.
469–475 Holloway Road
London N7 6LE
tel: 020 7561 7300
email: enquiries@cosprop.com
www.cosprop.com
*Specialists in the hire and
making-to-hire of period costume*

Re-enactment Supplies
Edward Street
The Leys
Tamworth
Staffordshire B79 7QU
tel: 01827 705433
www.re-enactmentsupplies.co.uk
*Suppliers of a range of arms and
armour*

The Knight Shop
The Knight Shop International Ltd.
Mochdre Commerce Parc
Colwyn Bay
Conwy LL28 5HX
tel: 01492 541300
www.theknightshop.co.uk
*Medieval plate armour, bucket boots,
clothing and weaponry*

Tirelli Costumi
Via Pompeo Magno, 11/b
00192 Roma
Italy
tel: +39 063211201
www.tirelli-costumi.com

US

Fall Creek Suttlery
917 E Walnut Street
Lebanon
Indiana 46052
tel: (765) 482-1861
www.fcsutler.com
*American civil war clothing and
accessories*

Jas. Townsend and Son, Inc.
133 N 1st St
Pierceton IN 46562
tel: 1-(574)-594-5852
www.jas-townsend.com
*Clothing and other goods
appropriate for 1750–1840*

Western Costume Company
11041 Vanowen St
North Hollywood
CA 91605
tel: 818-760-0900
www.westerncostume.com

Accredited courses

UK

Anglia Ruskin University: BA (Hons), Film, Televsison and Theatre Design
The Central School of Speech and Drama: BA (Hons) Theatre Practice
Central Saint Martins College of Art & Design: BA (Hons) Performance Design and Practice
Dun Laoghaire Institute of Art, Design & Technology*: BA (Hons) in Design for Stage and Screen
Edge Hill University: BA (Hons) Design for Performance
University of Leeds: BA (Hons) Performance Design
The Liverpool Institute for Performing Arts: BA (Hons) Theatre and Performance Design
Nottingham Trent University: BA (Hons) Theatre Design
Rose Bruford College: BA (Hons) Theatre Design
Royal Welsh College of Music and Drama: BA (Hons) Theatre Design
Trinity College: BA (Hons) Theatre Design & Performance
University of Wales Aberystwyth: BA (Hons) Scenography & Theatre Design
Wimbledon College of Art: BA (Hons) Theatre: Design for Performance
The Arts University College at Bournemouth: BA (Hons) Costume with Performance Design
Birmingham City University: BA (Hons) Theatre, Performance and Event Design
Buckinghamshire New University: BA (Hons) Spatial Design

Croydon College: BA (Hons) Design and Craft for Stage and Screen
Edinburgh College of Art: BA (Hons) Performance Costume. (SBTD Affiliate Organisation Member)
London College of Fashion: BA (Hons) Costume Design for Performance
Northbrook College: BA (Hons) Theatre Arts
Wimbledon College of Art: BA (Hons) Theatre: Costume Design
Wimbledon College of Art: BA (Hons) Theatre: Costume Interpretation

Accredited Technical arts courses:

UK

The Liverpool Institute for Performing Arts: BA (Hons) Theatre and Performance Technology
Royal Conservatoire of Scotland: BA Technical Production Arts
Wimbledon College of Art: BA (Hons) Theatre: Technical Arts and Special Effects

US

Boston University: BFA in Costume Design
Brandeis University
North Carolina School of the Arts
Ohio University
Rutgers University
Temple University
University of Arizona at Tucson
University of Florida at Gainesville
University of Illinois at Urbana
University of North Carolina at Chapel Hill
University of Texas at Austin

Index

Acknowledgements

To Michael Maxwell Steer, who had the initial idea for a book on the history
and practice of costume design – this wouldn't have happened without you!
To friends and colleagues Charlotte de Veaux and David Renoso for letting
my use their information and illustrations about 'mood boards'. To the brilliant
Costume Shop, Old Globe Theatre, San Diego, source of many of the images
in this book.

Picture Credits

© Alamy, pages: 26, 27, 28, 30, 33, 131, 180, 200.

© Arenapal, pages: 4, 23, 32, 38, 41, 53, 60, 61, 62, 84, 96, 98, 117, 132, 140, 141, 163, 167, 208, 211.

© Birmingham County Council, page: 35.

© Bridgeman Art Library, pages: 18, 20, 21, 22, 52, 145, 160, 179.

© Catherine Ashmore, pages: 213, 214, 216.

© Deirdre Clancy, pages: 1, 2-3, 6, 8, 9, 11, 25, 36, 39, 40, 44, 45, 46, 47, 49, 54, 55, 56, 57, 59, 63, 64, 66, 67, 68, 70, 71, 72, 73, 74, 75, 76, 77, 78, 79, 81, 82, 83, 86, 88, 89, 90, 93, 94, 95, 97, 100, 101, 102, 105, 106, 107, 111, 112, 113, 114, 118, 119, 124, 134, 139, 141, 150, 151, 153, 156, 158, 172, 173, 175, 183, 186, 187, 188, 189, 190, 191, 192, 193, 194, 195, 196, 197, 198, 199, 201, 202, 203, 204, 205, 206, 207, 209, 210, 211, 212, 214, 215, 223, 224.

© Getty Images, pages: 7, 37, 85, 104, 109, 110, 129, 130, 174, 182, 185.

© Mary Evans Picture Library, pages: 10, 12, 14, 16, 17, 19, 24, 29, 31, 50, 51, 65, 103, 126, 128, 136, 138, 142, 143, 152, 161, 164, 165, 166, 169, 170, 200.

© Science and Society, page: 15.

© The Kobal Collection, pages: 42, 43, 69, 116, 122, 125, 139, 146, 148, 154, 157, 171, 176-7, 181.